Not Exactly Don Juan…
And The Liberated Woman

Jody-Lynn Reicher
Foreword by Peter V. Dell'Orto
Cover Illustration by Toby Yu Min Reicher

Jody-Lynn Reicher

Special Acknowledgement
Pictures by

Karl Anderson
Josephine Dvorken
Brody Hall@cmail.com
Bruno Correa McKee
New Breed Fighters
Toby Yu Min Reicher
Joe Rossi
Sanskrit Photography

Consult to Peter V. Dell'Orto... Thomas Pluck

In Memory of
Leif Mickens,
Fighter Extraordinaire

Contents

Figure 1. Phil's Gym Las Vegas 2016

Introduction

Who would think being in a cage would set free you?
Yet, if we look at life, quite often we are caged within
perhaps, our own paradigm paralysis. We are controlled
initially by our tribal influences; then perhaps by our
cultures. Our siblings, and their influences may even
control us. And then we begin to really feel our '*oats*' of
being an independent individual, breaking away from
family, and parental conformity. What then do we
actually do? We follow our peers.

We don't solely create our own culture. Well, we do.
But most of us really don't. Why? It's too
uncomfortable. Everyone, deep down wants to belong to
something. Many will quite often choose a 'good' label
to be associated with, usually. However, there are those
times when someone portrays such a level of non-
conformity, which wouldn't be criminal, yet is quite
often condemned.

It is condemned not because it is illegal. Yet, it is
because it is different. Even with a slight paradigm shift
away from the norm of society or from their own culture,
the person may receive '*head-shakes*' that they never
thought would occur. Especially for a woman, the tribal,
and societal repercussions of '*breaking away*' from the
family morays and norms are great.

The funny thing is, from my personal experience,
women condemn women first. The older can be the
harsher. Why? Perhaps, it is because they've been
following the tribal creed longer. Which may have
become embedded into such a paradigm, that it is harder
for them to shift in their thinking. And also, they are

perhaps deep down jealous, that they didn't have the fortitude to step out of the box themselves.

Age, religion, race, color, and gender quite often are the basic variables we deal with in our societal, and tribal influences. When we cross the age barrier, its novel. When it comes to sports, it's often considered 'cute' if you don't have young children. If you cross the line of your religious upbringing, well then it can be hidden to a degree. But deep down there are always rumblings. Especially if you really understand more than both sides of the fence of the religions involved than the others do.

Crossing the race line is more obvious. Some people coming from a homogeneous background may often have a tougher time with a mind-set. Those brought up in a more colorful tapestry might have less of a problem in accepting a paradigm shift in race. This quite often concerns culture, and perhaps religion as well.

However, the final paradigm shift, gender is like "and the fifth little piggy went to the market." Instead of, "wee-wee all the way home". It is way out there. Stepping over that line turns to 'critical-mass' in a woman's mind. Then there is immediately the *nose-turned up* condemnation from within the tribal, and societal ranks.

An example would be:
    A woman going into a male dominated sport thought for combat. This may be what many consider, as my husband said, "…Conquering the last male bastion".

Such an example as mentioned above, was not the original intent of my seeking out self-defense skills from Grandmaster, Phil Dunlap.

As I've grown to understand most of us are told not to judge, and not to be judgmental. All the judgments that we are initially preached to '*not to do*', we start doing immediately. This is because quite often what we are told not to do, we are not always taught how not to do.

It seems as though when a mentor, peer, or another influential figure accepts the judgment from us, the judgment continues. We continue to judge, and most the time, it appears that the people we surround ourselves with, agree with it. So that may help us seal our paradigm on judgment.

As the reader will see, this story unfolds into a natural progression of change. Change in the writer's perception, and change in the Grandmaster's teaching, and thinking of a woman, as a fighter. It then appears the writer's husband sees what someone who isn't in the fight gym, sees. The Grandmaster sees it too, that is there no different from the men who want to fight, and the woman he is training in self-defense, wanting to fight.

As this book progresses, the molding, and shaping of two personalities continues to evolve. It appears as to the point where there are no differences between a man becoming a fighter or a woman becoming a fighter. In the end, fighting is not gender specific, as many would have believed or believe. Yet it is a choice for a variety of reasons.

As the author of this book to the readers, the dynamics of the time, the presence of minds that are thinking congruently and the doors opening for womens combat sports. The timing couldn't have been more perfect.

Plenty of obstacles had to be overcome. Especially when it came to how match-makers, promoters, referees, judges, athletic commissions, medical staff, audiences, other coaches, fighters, family, friends and the community would do everything to deter Phil and I from the process of getting me fights.

At times the world seemed against us. Phil would say that I had to understand that no one would agree with me on wanting to defend myself. No one would agree with me on learning how to fight in any capacity. This was due to my age, a woman, my being a mother, and my size. Phil would say, "As long as your husband is okay with it. And you can be a Mom and conduct business first, then fight second. I don't have a problem with it."

Foreword

Let me tell you about my friend, Jody-Lynn. And how I met her, and what training with her is like.

I met her at the house of Phil Dunlap, many years into my martial arts training and a few jam-packed years into my MMA training.

I had found Phil's while doing research for a role-playing game book. Unlike 100% of the other schools I contacted, he invited me up. I trained for a few classes over as many weeks before getting on a plane for Japan, where I'd be teaching English. Phil even went as far as finding the local MMA gyms for me before I'd even arrived so I knew where to look to train.

I once said something to the effect that Phil's school was one-third cops, one-third criminals, and one-third people wondering, "What am I doing here with all of these cops and criminals?" That third group had a wide variety of people in it. An up and coming writer, a comic book artist, a personal trainer, and myself – just someone who liked to train hard and who liked sparring in karate class more than belts, bowing, and kata and seen that turn into a series of amateur MMA fights.

People came and went. Lots of would-be fighters would come and leave when they found out how training could really be. It took a special sort of person to stay there, although generally no one would have regarded himself or herself as special. It's not that it was so harsh or tough, although it could be that. It's just that it was an environment where you were expected to both fend for yourself and look out for your fellow trainees. A place where you'd hit and get hit. A place where you'd need to put in the work but could feel safe to come and work when you didn't have that much work in you that given day.

Even within that group, Jody stood out. She was the smallest by far. I met her after I'd returned from Japan a few years later. She was also one of the toughest, if not *the* toughest, by far. Physically tough but also emotionally and mentally tough.

She got called by a lot of names. Jody. Jodes. Rainman, for her incredibly specific memories of how and when she'd met people ("It was a Thursday class, it was raining, and you, Felix, and I were the only ones there.") I referred to her as the Terminator. It's not a nickname that stuck, but it fit. You simply had to contain her until someone told her to stop, because she'd keep going. I could beat her in a match just out of sheer physical mismatch, but I'd die in a fight against her. At some point, I'd give up or hesitate or just get tired. Jody wouldn't do either.

There is a Japanese proverb – *nana korobi ya oki* – which means, "fall down seven times, get up eight." That's Jody.

I still remember Phil yelling at people hesitant to unload on her, "Hit her, goddamn it!" Or guys who couldn't bring themselves to open up a full-power shot on a woman – Phil would yell, "She's not a woman, she's a Jody!"

I knew from personal experience you had to drop any reservations you had going with her. She hit harder than anyone her size I'd ever worked with, and hit at least as hard as a Japanese buddy of mine who fought professionally at the same weight class would. You had to get in on her and land blows and never let up. You had to put them in hard and often. You couldn't give her an inch, a second, or a moment. If you did, you'd get grabbed and pounded with a rain of uppercuts, crosses, straights, and hooks until you finally either gave in or landed a wild blow and forced her to give you space. It was a matter of respect – of treating her like the fighter she is. But it was also a matter of survival.

Jody's more than a tough opponent, though. She's a tough training partner. She'll push you and critique to a literal millimeter. No bad reps, bad stances, or bad guards allowed. She can push so hard you need a break just because you don't have that laser-like focus that she can put into every training session. To this day, if I get a black eye in training, people who know both Jody and I immediately ask, "Is that from Jody?" Usually it's not. In fact, I can't remember her ever giving me one. But that's how people think of her – the toughest person I'd be training with.

But Jody isn't just a fighter. Her life isn't solely about training. Despite running more miles in a day than most fighters run in a week, and putting in solo time training *and* coming to class and outworking most of the class, nothing else ever slips. She is home to make breakfast for her kids and get them to school, no matter how early that means she has to get up to run. She doesn't miss an appointment at her office and squeezes in people who need treatment . . . somehow. And she's home for dinner and helps her kids with their homework and is involved with their school. Add in a strong relationship with her husband and assorted pets and you wonder why you can't seem to get half of that done.

A description of her would still be incomplete without mentioning her sense of humor. She does impressions. She tells jokes – usually really bad ones. That's not a problem because at least half the time she can't get to the end of the joke without laughing so hard she can't continue to speak. You don't even know why the chicken crossed the road this time.

You just know when she stops laughing, it's time to bring your gloves back up to your face and be ready to train hard. Because, Jody will be. ----*Peter V. Dell'Orto, April 12th, 2017*

And it struck me...All the children are pretty.
"How Do We Protect the Pretty Children"

As the canary sings,
Unsafe mines closing in.
How do we protect,
The pretty children?

To protect them,
We care and embrace.
We hold them in charms,
And we pray for grace.

We know not when,
To let them go.
For growing up fast,
We wish it were slow.

In times of now,
Appears so rough.
As we enter a time,
My Pretty children, it's tough.

Breaking through,
The monotony of lies.
And crashing through,
Political ties.

How do we protect,
Pretty children from sin.
When females are enslaved,
Our scruples caved in.

Chapter One
In The Beginning

As I received word that the person who'd attacked me in 1991 was being released early, I scrambled as to what to do. Others and I had done our jobs in writing letters to the parole board of the State of New Jersey, only to not have the State heed our outcry. Thus, having the State release the violent criminal early.

I'd spent hours upon hours after writing the parole board, and hoping that they wouldn't release him. Then prepared for when he would seek me out to finish the job. I made certain I had enough insurance to cover not just myself on short-term and long-term disability. Yet also made certain my entire business, including clientele, would be taken-care of if the worst were to happen to me.

After securing child-care in case of my absence, as well as increasing my insurance. I proceeded in getting three additional practitioners to cover my business, just in case. This would be so my clients wouldn't suffer much in my absence.

I alerted my babysitters in being cautious, knowing they might just leave me for fear of what could occur. I alerted a few relatives who lived close by, who could also help with child-care, and a couple of nearby neighbors. This would be so they could be there for my husband, just in case it all went down in a nasty way.

I'd just finished my biggest charity venture. It was the beginning of May 2008, I made the call. Phil answered, "Hello?"

I responded, "Hey, Phil it's Jody-Lynn Reicher."

He responded, "Oh hi. What's up?"

I replied, "Well, I have a little situation I need help with. And I don't want anyone to taken care of it for me. That's not the reason why I'm calling. You remember the thing I told you about in 1991?"

Phil responded, "Yes."

I continued, "Well, they let the bad guy out fifteen years early. He will be moving within six miles of my home. Train me."

Phil said, "Oh no. How did that happen?"

I responded, "Well, I really don't know. There were plenty of us that wrote the parole board. The prosecutor called me about three weeks before his release in April. I feel the prosecutor didn't complete his job on this case."

Phil replied, "That's terrible."

I responded, "Yes. The prosecutor offered to put a car outside our home. I turned it down. That's ridiculous. And I'm not getting a gun, a vicious dog or a new security system. I'm not changing my running either. And now I have two children, and we are in the middle of a third adoption. So train me, train me. I need to survive this. I don't want anyone taking care of this for me. Cause I know he is coming. I'm ninety percent certain he will make an attempt to finish the job. My goal is to finish it if he attacks again. Before he finishes me."

Phil replied, "Okay, sure thing. When would you like to start?"

I responded, "Right now, I just finished a big running charity event and I'm mentally fried. And physically I feel sick and very weak. So how about first week in June?"

Phil replied, "Okay. What time can you do?"

I responded, "I could do something after work on a Wednesday night, like about eight-thirty."

Phil relied, "Can we make it nine? I have a client ending just before then."

I responded, "Okay I could do nine at night on a Wednesday. I'll double check with Norman."

Phil said, "Okay, let me know."

I responded, 'Put me down for Wednesday June 4th at nine at night, and I'll call you tomorrow if I can't be there."

Phil replied, "Okay."

As I got off the phone, I could feel the positive energy of having made the phone call to Phil. I realized, he truly understood what I felt I needed to do. Although I was a bit petrified, because I knew his training would be tough. However, I also knew it would be accurate for what I might need.

I felt that I now was cultivating the ultimate responsibilities a person could perform. I had notified two local police departments. One I worked in and one I lived in. Dr. Dan Schaefer had suggested I do so, to not only protect the community because we felt the man being released was someone who was a person who struck upon given an opportunity. So in maybe becoming frustrated with not being able to get me soon enough, he may just go after a more unsuspecting new victim and then finish the job.

The phone call to Phil was the final piece that completed what I felt was necessary to protect our children, the community, and myself. Although I felt that I was the main target, and it would be me the criminal would come after. I realized that I had to think beyond my own boundaries as well.

Now it was time to wait, and hope that nothing would occur till I had proper training with Phil. When all the pieces were put into place I then had to contend with what others thought who were friends, acquaintances and relatives. And of course many verbalized that I was being silly. However, the people who didn't think I was being silly, were psychologists who knew the case, some law enforcement officials I knew, my husband, my secretary at the time, and Phil Dunlap.

Even as everything to protect and help our family and myself were in place, I began to have nightmares of what could happen. Waking up at times in a cold sweat, from hearing bad news in my dreams from what further damage the release of this criminal would cause.

My Brother's Keeper

I am my brother's keeper,
Water not blood is much deeper.
I feel the strain,
Beneath the grain.
As patterns grow more steeper.

If you can recall,
What has befalled.
There are those you find,
And in a bind.
Old friends you thought were cheaper.

When you change,
Some friends arrange.
Thinking their too smart,
Ways to push apart.
Ones you find are keeper.

And when you dare,
To show you care.
They pierce your heart,
With every dart.
And then arrives the reaper.

When chips are down,
Those who say 'friends' will frown.
Within your life,
They cause your strife.
Unfriends wish death on keeper.

Jody-Lynn Reicher

When I'm my brother's keeper
I will not be the cheaper.
I stay loyal to end,
My heart will not bend,
Because I'm my brother's keeper.

Chapter Two
Don Juan…?

The name Don Juan which was used by author Carlos Castaneda in many of his books, is used here as a matter of figurative speaking. It was a name selected by Carlos Castaneda in his writings and books on *Nagualism*. It was used to describe his varied experiences from a spiritual teacher of Mexican and perhaps, also Guatemalan descent.

As Phil Dunlap is not exactly Don Juan. As some friends and acquaintances would put it, *'Phil Dunlap is a colorful guy.'* Phil stands at about six feet two inches tall. Depending on when you're seeing him, during this writing time period he weighed about 168 to 178 pounds.

Phil Dunlap, a Grand Master in the Martial Arts. Phil is primarily a Grand Master in Burmese style martial arts of *Hkyen*, meaning "all out fighting." The Burmese call it *'Thaing.'* Phil has a broad range of understanding of the aspects of many areas of *'htwi hkyen'* (*'lethwei'* in Burmese), *'gamu hkyen'* (*'naban'* in Burmese) and other forms of martial arts for sport and self-defense.

Phil was trained from age six and forward by his now deceased maternal grandfather, William O'Shaunessy, they called him 'Wild Bill'.

Phil has always been straight with people. He even tried talking guys out of fighting. Because like he would say, "Fighting is crazy. Don't you know that?" You would stand there and look at him and wonder why is this guy who some called, *'The Crazy Guy in the*

Basement', just dissing the very thing he trains and has done for most of his life?

One thing quite a few people don't know about Phil is, that he is shy. But he fakes not being shy pretty well. Practice I believe. It's like me faking normal. Phil knows I try to do that 'normal' thing.

Phil has his own 'Phil'osophy. It's practically like any other philosophy I've ever learned, yet similar to my thinking. You have a question? He will answer it in his own 'Phil'osophical way. For example: Someone might ask, "Getting kicked in the legs. Ha. What's that's going to do? I mean, really."

So one day Phil is training at a local gym and this big burly strong man, who was in tremendous shape. The man weighing was an extremely and muscular approximate 250 pounds, he says to Phil, "I just don't see how a leg kick could hurt me."

Phil replies, "Well it can be crippling. If you throw a leg kick correctly at even the legs and it lands right. Well, it can really stop somebody. It's damaging if done correctly."

The muscular weight-lifting man in the gym basically now decides he wants Phil to try a leg kick on him. Phil asks the man if he is certain about this. The muscular weight-lifting man says, *'yes'*. Seemingly figuring, *'how could someone smaller than I, hurt me by kicking my thigh?'*

The muscular weight-lifting man asks for a demonstration from Phil. Phil being a kind, logical, and a complying individual, obliges. Phil addresses the man, making certain the muscular weight-lifting man is ready for a leg kick. Then Phil launches the leg kick, "Whack!"

Not only did the muscular weight-lifting man feel the leg kick at that moment, he also felt it that day, all day, and well, days after. Word had gotten around after that, in the gym that leg kicks were painful. The next time the muscular weight-lifting man saw Phil at this gym, he admitted that leg kicks were brutal, and now understood how effective a leg kick could be.

This was not the first time, nor the last, that someone would question Phil Dunlap on the validity of proper leg kicks. But it was probably one of the most entertaining.

Phil is the kind of guy that if he asks you to work with someone, or spar with someone you don't say *'no'*. Not because he would get upset, because Phil wouldn't get upset. But because Phil usually knew what he was putting you through, and figured what was best for your personality, your growth, and the learning of what you stated you came into his basement fight gym for. And Phil does not want to disappoint a soul. It's obvious he cares. And that has been his way of showing that he does, since I've known him.

Phil will do back-flips not just for his fighters. Yet also, for just the regular training guy that entered his fight gym. Phil has rules. One he holds near and dear is you don't abuse anyone. You don't hit your spouse, male or female.

Phil does not care what your religion is. He does not care if you did or did not find God. He does not care what your ethnicity is. He doesn't care what race you are. He does not care how you identify yourself. He does not care if you are homosexual, heterosexual, bisexual, etc…

Phil does not care if you have a rap-sheet. He does not care what you do for a living. Although, Phil would prefer you to made an honest living if you needed to pay bills, and survive, etc.. He does not care how you vote. If he gets a fight for you, he does care how you train, so you can be safe and successful in the cage or in the ring.

Phil does care if you're screwing up your life with drugs, alcohol, gambling, foods, or not keeping certain obligations to your children. Phil believes in 'put up or shut up'. Phil believes he must let you know when you've stepped over a line in the gym. That's his job.

Phil does not try to insult anyone, yet he is honest as the day is long.

Try or Be Dead

She bled through the night,
With some fright,
She knew not what lie ahead.

The hours did wane,
Not revealing the pain,
Of what many others had said.

She knew to fight through,
Being painlessly clued,
To those who feared to tread.

She said to her coach,
I'd rather approach,
So I must try or be dead.

Chapter Three
The First Test

Phil had me work private sessions three Wednesdays in a row. So here we were Wednesday June 25th, 2008 just before we started the fourth session. Phil asks me, "So what are you thinking?"

Smiling I replied, "Well…" I pause. I'm so afraid to admit that I'm actually enjoying the process of learning Phil's method self-defense. Albeit, scared of what Phil may think of next. I respond, "I don't know how to say this. But a…it's like I feel …" I shrugged. "Like I um…" I can't find the words.

Phil responds, "How do you feel?"

I try once more to respond, nearly laughing, "I think I kind of… Okay I know this may sound weird. But um…"

Phil says it for me, "Oh, it makes you feel *alive*."

I respond, "Yeah. That's it! But I don't get it. Is that weird?"

Phil asks, "Does it feel right?"

I reply, "Oh yeah. It feels right. Why?"

Phil replies, "If it feels right. Then it is right. And many guys have told me that it makes them feel *'Alive'*. That's not a bad thing." Nodding I agree.

Phil then asks, "Can you come in Saturday?"

I responded, "Yeah, let me check with Norman. But I'll be in. What time?"

Phil replied, "We start at ten in morning." I nod *'yes'*, in response.

Soon enough it's Saturday morning. I arrived at Phil Dunlap's Basement Gym at nine forty-five. There were three men already there. More were gradually arriving. I stand back to one side and corner of the room, awaiting what Phil wants me to do. I felt as normal as a hermit would in a room that begins to become crowded, *out of place.*

At ten o'clock Phil announces, "Everyone this is Jody. Jody this is everyone." I thought, *'I love the formality. It's very neuter. So they won't recognize the gender difference. Works for me'.*

Then Phil says, "Jody, this is John." John and I shake hands. Supposedly John is a police officer. He's about six feet tall and built pretty solid, about double my weight. He seems about age forty-one or so. I figure, *'this would be a good size to work with.'* John seems pleasant, yet a little apprehensive.

As Phil instructs John as to what to do. I can tell John really wants to help, but can't bring himself to acting criminal like. Phil witnesses this too. I thought this could be a problem as Phil was testing me. Not thinking that this could happen. Fighting and training men in self-defense is much easier than fight training, and or self-defense for a woman. Sometimes it's the person who's been victimized who it may be difficult for. Things reminiscent of an attack may invade an open-minded thought process of an individual training for self-defense, even if it is for their own good. However, this was not the case.

The situation Phil and I ran into, was that the person portraying a criminal may be afraid of being too rough with someone they did not know. As much as Phil explained what we were going to do, and had previously asked John for his help which he seemed per conversation with Phil a willing participant.

When John was faced with the reality of actually role playing a criminal, you could tell it did not sit well with him. Phil was a slight disappointed. I was at first, then I realized John had probably never attempted to role play like this with anyone other than a man, or even perhaps his own buddies in law enforcement. So John's reaction was logical. It was obvious John couldn't overcome his preconceived notions that now perhaps no longer held true.

So Phil moved me to work with Damien and Little Kyle. Damien was over 200 pounds, strong, with a wrestling background, and had no visible problems role-playing. Kyle was small yet knew how to attack fast. Their method of attacking showed me different ways for me to handle different attacks by different sized men. It was perfect. And yes indeed, my counter-attack was aggressive enough where it brought up the level of just how violent an attack could be. If anyone of the three of us would know, it would be me.

We asked Phil was there anything I should not attempt to do. I would attempt to bite, but not if I thought I would permanently damage someone in training. Such as taking off an ear with my teeth would be haphazard to truly apply full out in practice. These were just some ideas that had gone through my head many times. I was unique in that. Phil said that most men and definitely most women would be turned off by even thinking to make such a vicious counter-attack. My nature was different.

Jody-Lynn Reicher

Not My Daughter...

Not my daughter,
Not my son.

What has happened,
Can not be undone.

Whether ego, jealousy, or disregard,
Yet guilty that they know.

Now her parents,
Won't see her grow.

If people cared,
A life in their hands.

Not one confessed,
To one who stands.

Others too busy sweeping,
Under rug.

Ostrich's head in sand,
No one to hug.~~

Some could've directed,
A victim they knew.

It wasn't THEIR DAUGHTER,
She's just a ewe.

Chapter Four
Why Would Anyone Pick On You?

My nature has been so different, that twelve years before I took part in two twenty minute segments of Phil's classes. It was in the summer of 1996, at a local gym Phil and I conducted our businesses out of. Phil saw I was automatically thinking high level of viciousness in retaliation of being attacked.

Phil saw in the one session of me being grabbed from behind that I'd turn fast, allowing myself to be pulled in. Then, if I couldn't head butt, nor knee to the groin; next was to bite whatever I could. This is what came natural to me, with no training.

So after being grabbed from behind by Phil in the 1996 practice I saw my only defense after turning into him, I began to attack with my teeth. He tapped. I attempted biting in the 1991 attack, which did throw the attacker off a bit. My feeling was that it frustrated him. It showed him I was willing to fight back and I wouldn't beg for my life; to the contrary, I became rather crafty.

Then in July 1999, while walking on sidewalks of what had been crowded during the week, of a seemingly pleasant downtown area of San Diego streets. The area was just blocks from where I was staying by the Marina, this one Saturday morning at seven fifteen there was desolation. At first I thought nothing of it. Then after a half-block past the railroad tracks I'd just crossed, I began to get a cold chill. Something was awry.

I'd ran through and walked in city streets of Detroit, Flint, Tampa, and a variety of other cities with some trepidation, however this was different. I began to see what was coming my way, two men. After I saw them harassing a woman and a man in a bus stop booth about a hundred feet ahead, they were now coming my way. There were no police cars. No one was on the streets other than the people awaiting the bus. As the two men were coming my way, I knew I was alone.

I said to myself and God, "You'll just have to forgive me. I'm not going through this again. There will be no trial. I will be unscathed and they might be dead. But I'm just done with this. You hear me?" The two men got closer. I said to God one more time, "Forgive me. I am determined, and I will be unscathed."

The two men begin to spread apart as they get closer to me. Both the men were about five feet nine inches tall, out of shape, weighing about 185 pounds each, probably twenty-eight years old. The brunette goes to my left. The blonde looked straight at me. The brunette is the leader he is the aggressor of the two. The blonde helps corral the potential victim.

The brunette goes to come into my left side. To distract me, he asks a question of what would be typical of the beginning of certain criminal acts. I stop my walk, then crouching down, I become fully aware of where my fanny pack, body position, and hands are. I then override him. I say, "I'm a crazy US Marine. You come within my personal space. I will rip off your head, and shit down your neck. Try me." That stunned them. It stunned the blonde so much, he stopped his approach I saw out of the corner of my right eye, as I faced the brunette to my left. I remained in the crouched position. I was ready.

In my mind's eye I saw blood. I saw body parts. I had already dismantled them in my mind, now all I had to do was finish the job physically, and I would stop at nothing. Not one part of me shook. I was quite confident like never before, that I would walk away unscathed. Their blood would be strewn on and around them, where I'd lay them. Simultaneously the brunette asks the distraction question, "Do you have a cigarette?"

I repeat myself, "I'm a crazy US Marine. You come within my personal space. I will rip off your head, and shit down your neck. Try me."

The blonde now has a panicked look on his face as I remain in my crouched position. He moves towards the brunette to pull him away from me, and says, "Hey, man leave her alone she's crazy."

I respond, "Yes, I am. I wouldn't mess with me."

The brunette curses at me. He's already frustrated. He's circling to my left to get an advantage. The blonde follows him. The blonde no longer feels safe, he follows the brunette. By the time I'm facing the direction I was headed towards class on the sidewalk, the brunette is cursing at me. The blonde is pulling at brunette man's sleeve in fear. After about a total of three minutes or so, the attack is thwarted. They left with nothing but what they came to me with. Their lives.

As I feel my adrenalin rush through my body, I begin to realize that just about six miles to my left was a Marine base. I'd been out and about running that week a few times, to get thirteen milers in. I had run up to the gates of the opening entrance into the base and ran back to the Marina.

This is the part Phil was afraid of about me. I stand my ground to a ridiculous level. An old Marine friend once said to me after the 1991 incident, "In front of God and everyone." I never knew what Bob, my Marine friend meant by that, until that day in July 1999. Now I did. I'd be damned if anyone was going to take what was mine, they'd have to be willing to die to do so. And only God would defend me. So that is how, and where I stood.

The Things She Did

Most wouldn't do the things she did.
She'd carve out hope when it was hid.
Some would tag along just to see.
What they hoped she wouldn't be.

There were laws to make her quit
Yet she lived her life as she saw fit.
There were friends of enemies,
Who blinded by greed couldn't foresee.

A strong-willed nature did she have.
Blessed by divine prayer that she gave.
As others sought her magic potion
Many thought free was the notion

As time passed the wise ones saw
That free to others was the draw.
They found that lazy was not her plan
When something moved her she took a stand.

Chapter Five
First Test Results (2008)

As Damien and Little Kyle role-played that day with me, I took some good slams and hits. I felt a tad bit mangled; but I refused to complain. I would have to adapt, and I would. I hoped I'd passed the test. Albeit my neck, and head were a bit bruised and tweaked, I was fine. It was actually very empowering, at the very least.

Both Damien and Little Kyle coached me as we went. As to what they would think would be effective in an attack. And it was also how to learn to take a fall or a slam as well. They let me know when I was telegraphing as to how I would counter attack too.

The next private session with Phil was Wednesday, July 1st, 2008 again at nine o'clock at night. I entered Phil's basement gym. Phil came down from upstairs. I asked, "So, how'd I do?"

Phil replied, "Well, you did better than I expected. The guys liked working with you. You freaked Damien out with your willingness to bite. He said, 'that's just nasty'."

"Oh good." I responded.

Phil continued, "I was a little disappointed in John though. He seemed as though he wanted to help you. But he didn't seem like he could or was willing to do it the way it needed to be done."

I replied, "Well, yeah. But I think it was difficult for him. He seems like a really nice guy and a really sensitive guy as well. I really think he was afraid to hurt me. We don't know what he's dealt with in his line of work as well."

Phil said, "Yeah, but in his line of work he should be able to adapt."

I replied, "Huh. Yeah well. So I thought of some things. The guys were so helpful. They had me thinking of different ways of an attack. So I wrote them down."

Phil, "Let me see."

I continued, "Well, I have a quick question first. This guy, I just don't think he's a knife or a gun type. This is personal. So I'm thinking a *Louisville Slugger*. What do you think?"

Phil responds, "Okay, let me show you, and tell how and why it would or would not be used." Phil walks over to the north side of the wall where the cage type fencing ends and only a part of the wall is now showing next to a walkway.

The walkway separates an approximately ten foot by ten foot boxing ring from that part of the caged wall on one side. The walkway around the boxing ring leads to the bathroom, and to a back patio-pool area. There's a black heavy bag that almost touches the floor, and hangs from the ceiling. When hit by anyone, it appears to barely move.

I have suspected that this particular heavy bag seems to have rocks in it. I never asked Phil what was in this heavy bag. I just know that every time I've touched it, I'd think to myself, *'I'd never want to kick that. That bag will break me.'*
Phil walks behind the heavy bag, then reaches behind the end of the cage type fencing. He's reaching behind and wiggling his arms up and down. At first I see a gun, knives of sorts, then he pulls out a *wiffle* bat.

Phil mumbles, "Its back here. Somewhere." Tossing the *wiffle* bat to the side. I stare at what I later realize are heavy duty fake knives, and a fake gun. They appear authentic.

Then Phil pulls out a *Louisville Slugger*. Talk about a man prepared for questions. Phil begins, "Now, first he has to have a *Louisville Slugger*. Then you have to be there."

I asked, "What are you saying?"

Phil responds, "This will be a crime of opportunity."

I respond, "Oh, so he won't come looking for me prepared with a *Louisville Slugger*? Cause I would."

Phil replies, "Probably not. But if there's one that just happens to be laying around there, then he will use it. He's an opportunist. It appears he's the type of guy that if the opportunity presents itself, then he will use whatever is around and proceed."

I ask, "Then what are my chances?"

Phil responds, "Let me just show you." Now when Phil says this, because I've known Phil since Sunday afternoon, December 18th, 1994. You always have to wonder, *'is this going to be scary? I hope that Phil knows I asked this with no harm intended for demonstration.'* Cause sometimes, Phil's thinking is more out of the box than mine is.

In showing me, Phil takes the a *Louisville Slugger,* and swings it at what would be just below where the hip socket of a person would be, yet onto the big black heavy bag. The noise is hellacious. Because, we both know that would be crippling. Then I think, *'how do I survive? Would I stay down? Would I crawl? I know I'd go for the kill, if I could after a shot like that.'*

Phil says, "So, the likelihood of him having a *Louisville Slugger,* is probably slim."

As I mentally dissect what damage that portion of the body could take. The pain level, etc... I reply, "Well, thank God. But how would I survive? Now that I understand, why he wouldn't use a Louisville Slugger."

Phil responded, "Yes. Also he may have to chase you to actually get you."

I reply, "Yeah, but I'm talking about me walking out of my office or to my car in the dark."

Phil responded, "Okay, then we will drill how you lock up, coming out of your office, and getting into your minivan."

I then ask, "Can I use a pen to defend myself? Because I've always felt proficient at using a pen for self-defense."

Phil responded, "Yes. That's a good idea."
I reply, "Okay good. Because, I don't feel comfortable using a knife, really. And I'm not into guns. I'd rather use everyday objects and become proficient at them."

Phil replied, "I'll eventually teach you how to defend yourself with a rolled up magazine."

I respond, "Wow, imagine me beating a rapist to death with a *Playboy Magazine*. That'd be something." I laugh.

Phil replied, "Now that would be funny."

I said, "Yeah, but kind of a weird prude like myself would be carrying around rolled up *Playboy* Magazines in my car ready for a rape attack." I snort laughed.

Then Phil says, "Okay let's work on where you'd grab, and bite if the opportunity presents itself. But we have to get you not to telegraph the bite. Because that will be a problem. That was the one thing we have to work on." I nod in agreement.

I am a Witness

I am a witness,
I do detest,
The problems I know too well.

The pain I feel,
Not one is real,
They tell me, 'I don't exist'.

I live among us,
My life's *profundus*,
Has opened my eyes so wide.

I scrape off the anger,
Too much tumult a danger,
I hope that love can persist.

I hear people cursing,
And children hurting,
They gather pains all abound.

I am a witness,
To much that is hideous,
If they only knew my silent sound.

Chapter Six
Finally, Putting a Pen to Good Use (2008)

Since 1986, when I realized there didn't appear to be much security on airplanes. I could say I didn't feel very secure in flight. Yet, I knew I had to get use to the idea of flying before running competitions, and restrain my nervousness about the lack of security. I was now traveling now more due to my increased racing to improve, and to make the 1988 Olympic Marathon Trials.

In contemplating such, I had decided that having writing implements was a big benefit whether on a plane or in a secluded area like an elevator. It was an everyday item, which I have nearly always carried with me. I was always worried I wouldn't have on me a pen to write with. And having one, soon became a comfort. It was then when I began to realize it could be used for self-defense. Who would expect a diminutive woman such as myself to even contemplate self-defense?

Although by 1986, I hadn't heard of many hijackings. I decided nevertheless, to always be prepared. Especially when traveling alone or being in a secluded location. I have always resolved that in order for one to be able to be of use to others, one first has to be secure in feeling, and have a will to see things through to completion.

I believe that my thought process of being willing to be overly observant majority of the time, was healthy and safer. To be willing to defend myself, regardless of the obstacles that may seem insurmountable before me. The thoughts are, that there was and is always hope.

A former corporate boss once said to me, "If it is to be. It's up to me."

For some ungodly reason at a very young age, I have generally been prepared. Realizing, as free as we are that too comes at a price. Our military and law enforcement personnel do what they can. But they can't be everywhere. That each individual has to decide, are they going to live scared? Or are they going to live prepared? I decided the latter.

So Wednesday night July 1st 2008, Phil and I began to tackle the tactical approach of using a pen for self-defense. Now this was my comfort zone. The best pens were probably the cheapest. I designed the handle with the cap of the pen to stay as one piece, permanently. I'd never thought of this before. I had only seen it as a sharp enough weapon for two uses. Writing and defending.

Phil gave me some ideas. I made a bra pen. I made a running pen. I made console pens. It was just ridiculously cheap, crude and easy. And again, it felt very comfortable. Phil would be in the middle of telling me something about anatomy and I wouldn't stop him, but he'd stop himself and say, "Oh, you know your anatomy." I'd nod politely and he'd continue.

One night Phil said, "Take all your valuables that would break, if thrown out of your pocketbook."

I rummaged through my pocketbook, removing my cell phone and a pair of sunglasses. "Okay, I'm good." I said.

Phil asked, "So everything that could break is out of there?"

I responded, "Oh yes. How do you want me to carry the thing?" For I could see what he was thinking was attacking while I carried a pocketbook.

Phil answered, "How you normally would."

"Okay." I replied.

"Ready?" He asked.

I replied, "Yes."

I pretended to walk along and mind my own business, holding my pocketbook. Phil came in for an attack. As Phil came in, I tossed the pocketbook away and countered the attacked. We practiced this over and over again. Phil would take different angles. The more we did, the more violent I would get.

After we had finished the drill, Phil said, "You're probably counter-attacking more vicious than he's coming in for the attack."

I responded, "Is that bad?"

Phil replied, "No, most criminals would not expect this."

I responded, "Well then, I guess that's a good thing. Right?" Phil agreed.

Next was, where would I aim on the body with my pen? Phil demonstrated what a '*sucking wound*' was. It was basically how to perform '*shanking*' with a pen. The areas best to insert into, then jog the pen in and out without pulling the entire pen out of the body, can cause much damage. I was always working on bodies that I knew pretty much where to perform this for its most effectiveness.

Phil said, "The guy may not even take full notice of what you're doing or how you're doing this. With his adrenalin rush, he may not even feel it. It will be too late when he does."

I replied, "Good. More time for me. I'll try not to kill him. Maiming this guy permanently, is better than killing him. He took so much from me. I'm sure I'm not the only one."

Then we practiced if the attack went well standing, how I'd insert the pen. We also practiced, if the attack went awry and hit the ground where the guy could get mount. If the pen were trying to be stripped out of my hand, how I would manage.

Phil then used a six foot plus burlap dummy he had made. I practiced stabbing and *shanking* with the pen.

Hard Life is Easier

"Sometimes a hard life is easier",
 Many heard her say.
"Not all have a good time of it,
Life can struggle all the way.
If you're ill at six or seven or maladies pursue,
Perhaps if you've made it out of it,
You'll know more than others too.
The pain you feel today at 50, if never felt, it's true.
It can conquer even the strongest men,
And keep them in the blue.
You need not witness any war,
To understand your fate.
But if you have not experienced hurt
Not all struggles do abate.
So a lesson to the lucky ones,
Good fortune I wish to you.
If there is no struggle in a life,
There maybe less quality to view."

Chapter Seven
I'm Now in a Pink Panther Movie (2008)

Phil started doing these attacks, out of nowhere. I really thought I would fail at the very least. Sometimes I almost laughed, because it reminded me of Peter Sellers in the *Pink Panther* movies. The scene that was representative the most was when his sidekick, Kato would try, and keep him sharp. Then Kato would attack out of nowhere. Kato would always fail at completing a successful attack, and the character Peter Sellers played would succeed in thwarting the attack.

However, for me it was the other way around. I was quite certain Phil would succeed in attacking majority of the time. I dreaded it, yet I wanted to learn. So came the day Phil said, "Okay I want you to pretend you're locking up for the night. So go to the front of the room where the cage door is." I complied.

I turned my back towards the entire basement gym room. And made believe the cage door was my office door as I would be locking it up before walking down the hallway. As I proceeded finishing up the pretend scenario of my ending the night at my office and locking up, Phil launched the attack.

Somehow I responded, as he grabbed me from behind. I had turned so fast this time, and I saw as we flew into the air, which I could not have predicted that I was to Phil's right side. I grabbed him back to pull my body close in for a counter attack of as much viciousness as I could conger up for such an attack.

My hands were wrapped around the left side of his neck. My right heel was facing the ground. My left leg was bent at the knee and hip and left foot was going under his right knee. My face was at his right shoulder. I responded so quickly in mid-air that as we landed on the ground, Phil on his back, his right hand around my left shoulder to my back. Phil had lost his grip on my neck and hair.

I noticed that as we began to come crashing down to the ground and I was on my left side, that the following was about to occur:

I would bite where it would inflict pain and I could hold the bite to the right shoulder, albeit aiming for the right ear, or right side of the face, preferably the cheek. Yet, I was missing my intentional aim. However, I thought fast in mid-air. I could not believe how quickly my mind calculated precision, and what to do in under one second.

Also, I saw my right heel was in the perfect position to do a hard heel kick to Phil's crotch. I went for both the bite and the heel kick to the crotch as we came crashing down. Success!!! *The Eagle has landed.* So I hoped. Albeit painful to my instructor.

After we crash landed. As we got up, I looked for approval of perhaps good pain inflicted. I hoped I passed the test. Phil initially got up like nothing had happened. However, I remember this man already had 114 fights in him, most *'no holds bar'* fights. Burmese style was groin kicks allowed. And he'd fought in Burma. He trained men, by letting them kick him in the legs probably 500 times a day and their weights ranged from 130 to 320 pounds. Mostly of his fighters were 147 to 210 pounds.

Phil had seventy-eight fights in Burma. In Burma the fighting is way different than Mixed Martial Arts in the United States. In Burma their *'no holds bar'*, includes head butting and groin shots. In Phil's basement gym, it is unmanly to complain about taking a shot to the groin once. It's an unwritten or unsaid thought. Or at least, I thought that way, which that's another story later in this book. This brief story below describes his sensitivity to the issue:

My knowing a story about a certain person who had much martial arts under their belt. They happen to be someone Phil thinks highly of. The story goes something like this. The man asks, "Phil, how do you take such shots to the groin? It's like it does not even effect you."

Phil responded as if quite simply, "Well, I take my boys and I place them on a counter. Then I take a Ball Pin Hammer and I begin tapping them. Each time I do it a little harder…"

The man was appalled, yet believed Phil. He came back the next week, and told him that he could not bring himself to do it. He felt quite wimpy. So he declared. Later the man found out that Phil was kidding.

Phil taught me to inflict more than one pain. Phil through his demonstrations with me, proved to me most people cannot handle what overwhelms the body. That is, pain in two places at the same time. I knew this because he demonstrated on me.

So as we had gotten up from the crash to the ground, Phil looked sore. He got up like he had been riding on a bronco all day long for the first time. As he walked over to get his 'traditional' one gallon water bottle for a sip, he said clearing his throat, "Uhhh , that was good."

I started to giggle simultaneously as he got up and walked over to his one gallon bottle of water. I had to control myself, because I could see I actually effected Phil. And I was quite surprised. It was beyond my belief. But it did show I was effective.

I then asked, "Really?"

Phil responded, "Yes. Very good."

I said, "Thank God."

There were other attack scenarios, such as the 'minivan attack'. You're locking up or unlocking your minivan, and then you're grabbed. You are opening your back hatch, and you're attacked. Then one night we did one that I felt pretty good about. It was the attack scenario inside the minivan, from behind.

Phil didn't realize I had followed through on creating weapons that fit in my console and other areas of the minivan I could reach. Yet the children couldn't reach them, and husband had no clue what I had done. After all this was over, I had to explain it to Norman.

So one night Phil says, "Okay. Minivan attack from behind inside."

We proceed outside getting our shoes on, and I unlock my minivan and he goes into the van. Then I lock the van. Then I do a retake, and unlock my van and stupidly pretend I don't know anyone is in the van. I get into the driver's seat, ready to start the car and he attacks me from behind, strangling me.

While I try to stop the choke from behind in tucking down, yet relaxing portions of my neck and head to keep the choking to a minimum. This is so I don't pass out or tap out. I quickly am able to pull out a modified pen and am ready to put holes in his plan. He stops.

"Good". Phil remarks.

I ask, "You didn't realize how intense I was about creating weapons where others couldn't see them. You know Norman does not even notice them. He has no clue what they are. They have two uses." I then proceed to show Phil all the places I've hid them. I also have a few other items. This is so, if I can't retrieve my hand-made weaponry for protection in my car, there are additional '*safety nets*' for my protection.

Chapter Eight
Trunk (2009)

Next was, *'can Jody get out of a trunk'?* One Sunday during the afternoon, Phil had me come in. He wanted to do trunk work. Oh, I should say, *'learn to escape'* from a few different trunks he'd lock me in, and then twice he'd have it where he would make certain that there was no lighting in the trunk
.

It was around one thirty in the afternoon, cloudy and damp. Phil says to me, "I see you're getting ready for him."

I replied, "Well, hey I'm just letting the world know I'm here. This is where I'll be. No one wants me to be free. However, I see freedom differently. I'm willing to meet my Maker. Is he willing to me his? I don't think so. He's a coward."

Phil replies, "Okay. Let me make you more ready."

I respond, "Okay, so what do you want me to do?"

Phil replies, "How 'bout I teach you how to get out of car trunks. Because, it's a possibility."

I respond, "Okay." At this point I am a little nervous. I'm thinking, *'how am I going to respond being stuffed in the trunk of a car?'*

After we fight, Phil grabs me, and carries me out to the garage. He then throws me into a trunk, and shuts the door. The effect of me getting my head whacked on the trunk, was actually unintentional. But I almost laughed because I thought, *'okay a little rough. But hey, perhaps this could be good preparation for the real deal'*.

I got out of the first one, with the trunk light on. Then we did it a second time in the same trunk, without the light on. I got out of that. Then we used another car trunk with no lights on, and I got out of that as well. Then we discussed kicking out the back seat, depending on the car model. After kicking out the back seat I would have an option. I told Phil, "I'll beat him silly."

It would be most logical to have him have to pull the car over and he would not expect me to do what I did. He would probably panic. If we were on a highway, I envisioned that I would run on the shoulder against the traffic and pray to God, he couldn't carefully get it together to chase me even with the car backwards on the shoulder fast enough than I might be able to find an *'off'* ramp or hopefully someone would rescue me.

I told Phil I'd rather stay and do damage then get out of the car if it were good odds of surprise on my part. However, you just never know how anything like this could go down. I knew to possum at points. I had done that during the initial attack in 1991. If needed this time I'd do better.

Chapter Nine
He's Dead (2009)

I did not start fight training for competition till March 25th 2009. I had to focus on the situation at hand that brought me to Phil Dunlap's Basement Gym. Meanwhile, my husband Norman was begging me to become a fighter. He'd heard stories, and such I'd come home and tell him how tough these men were at Phil's basement gym. He thought it was in me to become a fighter. I wasn't so sure.

In November 2008, after having a bout of kidney stones, a burst ovarian cyst, and a host of tears in my feet that year, from attempting 493 miles in six days on the road for charity in end of April. Them I attempted setting a record in early October 2008, to no avail. My regular running weeks ranged from ninety to two hundred and thirty miles a week. However, every time I went beyond one hundred eighty miles a week I would be losing my stomach on the road as I ran on my seventh day of the week that summer.

Of course all the attempts were at the wrong times when I needed to try, and land a good ultra-event performance. I had put in about 6,000 miles of running that year. I'd had so many foot and leg injuries, albeit I ran through them. I knew I'd torn part of my extensor retinaculum in December 2007.

It was on a early morning training run I was getting ready for a charity event that I was organizing for five charities. When I heard a pop, and felt the searing sharp pain at the top of my left foot going up a long, steep hill at about three in the morning. Going up Skyline Drive at

59

three in the morning is peaceful. Then later I traversed back over Skyline Drive, coming back over the top, coming back down the same side as I was returning home. Watching the sun rise as I ran, I then felt another snap from the top of my left foot at the crease. I felt lame. However, I had more than eight miles to go.

The first snap I heard and felt, evidently didn't cripple me as much. The second snap and pain halted me for thirty seconds to assess just how I'd flop my left foot down as I ran down hill for more than another two miles, then seven more miles of undulating territory to home.

It seemed nothing was going in my ultra-running direction. I was purely disgusted. And then after the parole board decided it was best to allow a violent predator out early. This was just as I was conducting and getting the charity run "The Out 'N Back of New Jersey" set for the last week in April 2008.

Then the debacles of that Ultra-running officials who trusted the same race director in Texas as was 2006, and 2007 for this same event. Now in 2008 again, had not picked a good course to qualify runners on for the United States Twenty-Four Ultra-running team. This event occurred in early November 2008.

After that, I was done with racing and running ultra-events for the time being. So as Norman practically begged me to quit racing, and start fighting for Phil; fighting in competitions became tempting. I always wanted to be a boxer, and I liked Olympic style wrestling.

So a week after Texas, it was now mid-November 2008. Norman said, "Go with my blessing."

I replied, "You know what you're asking?"

Norman smiled and said, "Go the whole way with this."

I responded, "You know these guys are really tough. I don't mind breaking my nose. But can you handle it? I don't want to hear 'what for'. You know?"

Norman continued to smile, "Yes. Go the whole way. Go with my blessing."

I replied, "Okay. I'll let Phil know this week, when I see him for a private session this Wednesday night. But I first must focus on self-defense. The guy is still out there."

A little over four months later I would get the call that would set my fight career in motion. As I had said to Phil, and he felt I was correct, "Phil he will begin to stalk or attempt the attack between March 21st 2009 and April 1st 2009. Then on March 18th 2009, I said, "He's coming for me. I can smell it. Spring is in the air."

Phil replied, "Yes. I believe you're right."

And then it came:

> On March 21st 2009, a Saturday, unbeknownst to me the criminal released on April 1st 2008 with the tier reduction on October 1st 2008 thus had moved into

his mother's home approximately six miles from my home. He had just died.

On Tuesday March 24th 2009, I received a phone call from a detective at my office. I called into work to check messages. While I took care of our youngest daughter, washing the bathroom and kitchen floors before going to work. I heard the detective's message to call her at home, or on her cell phone.

I called her and got her at home. She said, "Jody, he's dead." I was so stunned. She waited, "Aren't you going to say Hallelujah?!"

I responded, "Uh, I never wish anyone dead. How did this happen?"

She responded, "I don't yet know. I'll try to find out. He died Saturday, March 21st." We chatted for a while. Then I called my husband's cell, left a message. I called my sister and briefly spoke with her. Then I called my mother-in-law and kept the conversation brief as well. I called Phil Dunlap, and we spoke shortly. When the babysitter arrived I told her quietly, for I did not want to share it around my daughter who was wise at nearly three and half years of age. I called a Priest, whom I knew had been praying for me, and a Minister as well.

I left brief messages for them to just call me. When I got to work that afternoon, my secretary and I hugged. Then our phone rang. It was the Priest. I gave him the news. He responded, "...On Friday night I was praying before bed. Your name came up. And I asked God to 'remove this burden from Jody-Lynn Reicher'." Thank you Father. I think of that everyday. I am truly blessed.

Jody-Lynn Reicher

How She Became a Fighter

How she became a fighter,
No one really knows.
They said she had no power,
And that she was quite slow.

It was apparent to her husband,
For he felt that she could reap,
The benefits of fighting,
For it was *souly* deep.

He took approach one day,
For the matter was at hand.
He prodded and he poked her,
And he finally took a stand.

"You really should become a fighter,
I really think its you."
She responded already tired.
"I can't say if it's true."

She couldn't tell him what's inside her,
Yet the willingness would grow.
She continued to her husband,
"We're in the middle of adoption, so.
The answer is just 'no'."

As months passed and she planned,
To give the years running a go.
However, inner turbulence,
Would soon disrupt the flow.

The running year of 6,000 miles,
Was torturous indeed.
Calling down to Florida,
Some consoling she did need.

She got her Dante on the phone,
And he totally agreed.
The she would go a fighting,
It really was her creed.

So never looking back,
She'd double check with hubby.
So they'd remain on the same track,
Remaining lovey dovey.

When confronting her husband,
She really did exclaim,
"My insides are a leaping
It's something I can't explain.

He responded quite happy,
"I think you should go all the way."
She stated, "I really want your blessing.
That's what I'm asking for."

He stopped his guitar and answered,
"There's no need to implore.
I knew you'd be needing,
To finally explore."
She then asked him,
"Do you know what's in store?

For I'll come home all bruised and broken,
Could you accept me then?
We're quite a violent bunch,
You have not witnessed me fighting men.

As you've found I love to punch,
And wrestle to and fro.
And so I need your blessing,
So I can tell Phil, 'it's a go'."

Chapter Ten
She Won't Go Away (2009)

Phil started, "I told Scott Morgan of New Breed Fighters, 'I think I have a fighter. In the last two months she's broken her finger. She comes back in for the next class. Then she breaks her nose. I set her nose. And then she stays for the rest of the class still, and rolls. After that session she goes back to her office, and works."

"Then she gets cauliflower ear, they stitched her ear. She came back to the next class. Then she breaks and dislocates her ribs sparring with Dan, keeps fighting for twenty minutes till he nails her with a liver shot. Then she thinks she's a wimp, because the liver shot stopped her. She goes to stand up, and the ribs pop out. She wants to stay and work. But she couldn't move without pain. I told her that she was done for the night. She's upset that she can't get punched for a while."

Phil continues, "The next class she comes back in with an ace bandage, and says, 'I ran fifteen miles this morning. It was a little rough the first five miles I had to get use to breathing into the pain. Thank God today was Saturday, not Friday because I could've only ran five miles after Thursday night due to rib pain.'"

"She's at most classes. She's here Monday, Wednesday, Thursday, and Saturday. So the topper is, she comes in and has a mark on her arm. She asks, 'What's this?' I let her know its ringworm. She asks, 'What do I do?' I tell her she can't be in the gym till it goes away. She's bummed."

"Now get this. She got rid of it in twenty-four hours. Yep. She told me that she put a towel in her mouth and poured bleach on it. She calls me and says, 'I was so desperate. I think I killed it. You want to see it? I think it's dead.' She killed it in twenty-four hours with applications of bleach. I think I got a fighter. She just won't go away." Phil shakes his head looking at me.

I ask, "Who's this man?"

Phil responds, "Oh he's the promoter of *New Breed Fighters*. Our guys fight on his shows."

I wonder if I ever will get there, and get to fight on Scott's show. Now I remember guys getting ready for his shows. I'd yet to get to go to one. *'I must try and see how it all happens'*. I think to myself.

I decided awhile ago when I made the decision to switch from self-defense to fighting that I would be at Phil's group classes at least three to four days a week and maintain doing the Wednesday night privates with Phil as well. I decided this after I asked Phil, "What do you expect from your men?"

Phil replied, "I want them in here four days a week for amateurs and five days a week if you're a pro. The cardio you do on your own, that's your responsibility."

Chapter Eleven
First Face-Lock (2009)

One Monday evening in May 2009, Phil's basement gym was packed. There were about fourteen guys in all that night. Most of us were doing ground. There were three guys in the corner ten foot by ten foot boxing ring, doing *round robin.*

It was the seven o'clock class that went till eight-thirty. Then Phil would do his traditional, "Anyone want to roll?" Then the guys who had fights coming up, or wanted to test themselves would *'roll'* with Phil, till they tapped out, or were completely exhausted. Sometimes it was because they couldn't withstand the pressure. There were times people did get ahead of themselves. So they thought they would challenge Phil.

Phil made no bones about it. He would work with anyone. Phil would be Phil. He would at times appear to *'play with his food'*. Yet, intelligently Phil would *roll* or do *stand-up.* Phil knew well enough that he had to remember some new people wouldn't show all their skills the first or the second day or week they entered his basement gym. Really only Phil's fighters, and grapplers were the ones Phil expected to work with him after class.

About fifteen minutes late to the class in walks this twenty-something year old man. He was a kid who had been one of Phil's fighters. Guys say 'hi'. However, he was not very disciplined I found out later that night.

This was my first time meeting this young man, and I'd now been at the gym for almost a year. And I had

69

already competed in a grappling tournament and was getting ready for the next grappling tournament.

When Phil put this young twenty-something year old man with me, he looked none too pleased. The kid looked over his shoulder, and then looked at me. I introduced myself and put my hand out to shake his hand. He definitely did not want to work with a woman, about double his age, and seventy to eighty pounds lighter than himself.

I asked, "What do you want to work?"

He responded, "I don't know, what do you want to work?" He hadn't been in the gym in probably a year or so.

I call Phil over, "Hey, what would you like him to work, and what would you like me to work?"

Phil replies, "Have her work from her back. Try to pass her guard. Jody, go for submissions from your back."

I respond, "Okay, good." I look at the twenty-something year old kid, realizing he's just not use to me. I'll just flow with this. Every time a new guy would enter Phil's basement gym, Phil would have to introduce me as 'The Jody'. Kind of like an alien from outer space. Then they'd see I was cool, with however they worked. Although there were times that some men were reluctant.

Phil would see the reluctance, and show them by demonstrating on me, that I could handle what they could dish out. Or one of the other guys who were not new would work with me.

However, if that didn't work the following would occur if stand up was involved:

> Phil said, "Okay." As he strolled over to the bin, that had four ounce gloves in it of all sizes. Putting them on his hands, he'd say, "So, let me show you something..."

> I'd think, *'Uh Oh. Here comes the demonstration. I better cover up. No fear. No fear. Our Father... Oh St. Michael...'* And then whack... I'd grrrr. Body shot or two, punch to the head and if I wasn't lucky that night a kick to the leg.

> Then Phil would stop. "See, she can handle it." I respond, "I'm good. Give me ten seconds for you.",

Then usually what would occur was that the new guy got comfortable with the idea of trading with me. Eventually the new guy would realize that I could be a challenge depending on what they were working, and what level they had as far as grappling.

What would happen in both scenarios was that either the new person complied and stuck around, coming back for more future sessions. Then they'd either get use to me being present. Then they would want to work with me. Or they would last one, maybe two group sessions at Phil's, then not come back.

Then not coming back usually meant that they had either done something stupid or illegal on me to get me to not want to work with them. Like the one time a thirty-something year old tried to do a small digit (trying to submit a person by tweaking or breaking fingers or toes) lock on me, which is not taught for MMA or grappling in Phil's gym. Nor would it be legal in the UFC, NAGA, or any other big fight promotions. And it was not what we were supposed to be drilling.

Or as one guy did, in not allowing me to do a *takedown*, by grabbing the cage fencing, during fighting with me. This was so I could not do a *takedown* on him after landing punches. I found out he ended up in jail when I wanted vengeance, and wondered where this guy now was for the last week.

But mostly I dealt with them. Sometimes better than some of the original crew did who were there before I walked through the doors the first time. Phil knew I had a long fuse. I was friendly. I tried to make no assumptions about anyone. I just figured, 'everyone here is a great fighter, and would always be able to handle me'.

Then this one Monday night in May 2009 this twenty-something year old kid is trying to pass my guard. He's getting frustrated. He seemed talented. Then he decides he wants to try a face-lock on me. I'd never had it done to me, but when it was applied, I thought it to be painful, yet interesting. My face went numb on one side. The kid leaned all of his weight into his forehead onto the right side of my nose. Finally, as I was trying to decide how to get out of it and it was going numb, I then tapped.

I said, "Wow! That was powerful. What is that called?"

The kid responded, "A face-lock."

"Hmmmm. Hey, how do I prevent or get out of such a submission? That is quite effective." I wondered out loud.

Phil asks, "Question?"

I replied, "Yes. He just did this amazing submission on me. It's this face thing."

Phil responds, "Oh, a face-lock. You have to move your hips and it will ease."

I ask, "Phil could you show me?"

The kid now looking around like, *'who saw this?'* Meanwhile Phil is saying to the kid, "Pay attention to what I'm showing her. So you can drill it with her." Meanwhile, I feel a section of my face numb, yet I'm almost laughing because this guy thought I was going to freak out. Yet instead I pulled what my husband would call a, *"Spockette"* on him.

Before I know it, the kid says he has to leave. I'm thinking, *'Doesn't this young man have people who like him here? Who will work with him?'* The answer I found out would have been *'Noone.'*

I may have been numb for ten days after that, but I got a few lessons from it. First was, how to get out of that submission attempt, and then to do a hip switching drill more vigorously that Phil had shown me earlier in the year. Second was, the guys were accepting me versus now a younger, stronger man. And it had to do with his attitude, and their respect for the people who were in Phil's basement gym who were there for the right reasons.

I asked Phil later, "Who was this guy?"

Phil replied, "He was a fighter of mine. He was very talented. But he wasted it. He's a spoiled rich kid. He had a fight and could have won it easily, yet he disregarded my orders from the corner. I can't have that. He hasn't been in, in probably a year. I put him with you as a test."

I asked, "What kind of test?"

Phil responded, "To see if he could refrain from being selfish, and work a skill set for both of you."

I asked once more, "Did he?"

Phil replied, "Nope. He's still selfish. I don't need that in here."

I realized that I was not a problem. Phil had said that to me. "Remember, its people's own insecurities. It's not about you. It's about them."

Looking back over time, I have to say that is one of the most important statements made to me in my life, given to me by another human being. The way it was delivered by Phil over time. It now is one of the most important effective statements made to me, in order for me to really understand humanity, and cope with other people's realities. It is a statement that keeps me at peace.

Jody-Lynn Reicher

From Whence She Came

From whence she came,
No one could know.

Their judgment to blame,
Her fire did grow.

Wounds inside,
She did ignore.

She strives for happiness.
No one could cure.

They pursed their lips,
Their anger did floor.

Her outsiders did quip,
Understanding not what envy was for.

Insiders cursed,
And pleaded to her.

How could she do…
What they didn't plan to occur?

And because she defied them,
Her life would not be the same.

One day to her insiders,
She did claim.

"My life is my life,
Not yours to play.

I'll play on the mats,
The street, or the floor.

I'll choose to run,
To roll forever more.

Chapter Twelve
Preparing to Fight Men in Competition(2009)

In June 2009, Phil and I entered me into a grappling tournament. Due to my size, my age, my inexperience, and my cardio, we planned to enter me in as many divisions as possible including male and female categories. We needed to see me in different variables. The last tournament I had only three matches. No one was over thirty years of age. Not one woman was within twenty five pounds of me and all had more experience. And as usual sandbaggers there were quite a few.

At the time we were in a rush, because like the rest of the world, we thought age mattered. At this point, we were wrong, and so was everyone else. We realized this about three years later.

Phil, to prepare me for the upcoming tournament, one Wednesday night, June 10th 2009, decided to do something different.

Upon entering Phil's basement gym for a nine o'clock private lesson, Phil asks, "How you feeling?"

I respond, "Uh, Okay."

He continues, "We're going to do ten, three minute rounds on the ground". I knew it would be rough. I knew it would be painful. And that I'd have to withstand Phil's suffocating pressure, and not panic while losing air.

Phil was fantastic at keeping his weight down (pressure from leverage of maneuvering your own body-mass onto precise areas to keep your opponent at bay) in all top positions. Phil could do this to the point he weighing 178 pounds, at times he felt more like a 350 pound object on top of your ribs and chest areas. It was a matter of proper weight distribution. I worked on not tapping to suffocation. I knew I had a high level of endurance. I knew how to feel at ease, breathing extended, light breathes. And, I'd use it knowing I wouldn't pass out or die from a chest compression.

I'd learned how to control my breathing, and to use as little energy in breathing or movement when being crushed. The bonus of me being so small was that all the men in the gym were 135-300 plus pounds. And at that point I'd worked ground with most of them, if not all that had entered Phil's basement gym.

Something else I'd also worked on since I was a child, was *'possuming'*. I acted like nothing bothered me and *'playing dead'*. It was my strategy when I played *'war'* with my brother and the kids on the block. And I'd used it in an attack on me in 1991. So I understood its usefulness. I'd slow my heart rate way down, go limp, breath minimally without holding my breath.

Phil sets the timer for three minute rounds, with one minute rests. We begin in the standing position. Before I know it I'm on the ground. I'm on my knees trying to take him down. I error and am quickly reversed into an unfavorable position.

First round passes, its not so bad. I'm still nervous though. Then the ten second buzzer goes to start the second round. Again, after chasing Phil around to attempt a *takedown*, I get reversed. Phil pins me to the floor. My right shoulder can go nowhere. I wriggle like a fish with a hook in their mouth trying to get free. Before I know it, the round ends. This same pressure and response continues for five more rounds. Now I'm getting tired. But I won't let on.

By the beginning of the eighth round unknown to me Phil's has been increasing the pressure a little each round. He does not reveal this till the end. I wonder *'why am I so weak'* in handling Phil's suffocation in the eighth round. I figure I'm just so weak.

After the eighth round I wonder if I can handle any more pressure, especially his increasing pressure in having me in his scarf position. I'm afraid I might tap to something simple for fear. I might not have the mental fortitude to believe I can breathe through the pressure that Phil applies.

Before we begin the ninth round Phil says, "You're doing good. Two more rounds. It's not you. I'm increasing the pressure on you with every round."

I feel a sense of relief. I respond, "Okay, good." I still know it will perhaps be painful, but more so, it's scary to me. The feeling of fear, *'is how much pain is the suffocation versus feeling as if I am so pained. It's not suffocation yet a might be a rib or other damage. How will I know what is smart'?*

I now realize I have to trust my instincts. I know fear increases the rate of blood pressure, vasoconstriction, and heart rate. I think, *'If I can relax. I may be able to allow my body to bend, rather than break'.*

The ninth round begins, again Phil gets a dominant position on me. I'm dyeing. I'm doing everything not to panic. I cannot remember how I made it through the ninth round. Then the buzzer goes off, I have time to regroup.

He says, "Last one." I realize, *'I might make it.'* But I also realize, *'He'll put more pressure on me. I'm getting tired'.*
The tenth round buzzer goes off and we begin again for the tenth time. One thing I know is, he wants me to be aggressive. I come out as aggressive as possible. Me knowing full well before hand, that I will put myself in trouble. However, being so aggressive is the one thing I have left inside me. Phil wants to see what I have.
As the last round progresses, I know the test will soon be over. The round ends.

Phil says, "I told a couple of the guys that I was doing this with you tonight."

I responded, "Oh."

He continued, "You did good." I then thank Phil. We then go over some technique. Soon the private lesson is over.

Jody-Lynn Reicher

The Commitment

Men will say, ' I want to fight.'
 But in their head, they are not right.
They pose and drill
But lack the will.

They act as though they have time to kill
Time slips by as if to waste.
At thirty-five,
They're in a haste.

Where is the fighter,
We cannot see.
The man who came,
And claimed he'd be.

A dreamer, a player.
We know too well.
They'll train one day,
And not the next.

And wonder why,
Their fight plans vexed.
They look over the fence at me.
And think I have no injury.

I can't complain, I can not tell.
Why I desire to train like hell.
It's the compulsion of the fight you see.
I've learned it is what sets me free.

Chapter Thirteen
The Tournament (2009)

On June 27[th,] 2009, a Saturday, at the Mennen Arena in Morristown, New Jersey a grappling tournament was to take place. A Grappler's Quest Event, it is my second tournament. The setting was a hockey arena. The arena was chilly, even though it was a mild, sunny, summer day outside. Inside the arena you could feel the frigid cool air of the hockey rink we were to compete in.

That day Peter Dell 'Orto, and I got there around eight-fifteen in the morning. We arrived separately from our homes. He'd already had plenty various fighting experience in Japan. But ground was new to him. He'd not ever competed in ground as far as I knew.

Phil gave me instructions to weigh-in, and sign up for Men's Open Division (ages eighteen and up) Bantam Weight (120-129.9 pounds); Beginner (zero through eighteen months) and see if there were any Novice (zero through six months experience) categories at light weights for Men's Divisions as well. Women's Open Division (ages eighteen and up) lighter weights Novice, Beginner, and then when Phil would arrive, he'd figure which one's I should focus on.

Initially, they were not going to let people be in more than a few divisions. But when Phil arrived and spoke with man who ran the event, whom he knew he was okay with my doing multiple divisions and categories. I would just pay more. That was fine with me. We had a couple other people besides Peter and I competing on that day. They each did one to two categories; getting in one to three matches a piece.

By the time all was said and done, it was about two-fifteen in the afternoon, and I hadn't gone once. Yet, we had me signed up for five divisions/categories, including two or three Men's Divisions/Categories. We had me in the Men's ages forty to forty-nine, Beginner, 150-159.9 Weight Class. Believe it or not the Men's Divisions were the closest to my age, experience and one was sized nearer to my weight, compared with the women's divisions.

In the Women's Divisions, there was no one in Novice. There was no one my age, all were thirty-four and under years of age. Mostly twenty somethings in all the women's divisions, except the Expert Division.

Phil did want me to experience competing with the women. I had really no one to play with in training my size or my gender. Then all of a sudden at about two-thirty, my name got called. I had a match with a forty six year old man 150-159.9 pounds, in the beginner category.

I was now cold. I hadn't been warm in a while. I had however, been warmed up and cooled down multiple times when we thought I might be competing that day. Peter and I screamed for Phil. He was finishing coaching on the complete opposite end of the arena. The arena at this point was packed, and they had all the rings with matches going; which were about twelve matches all at once.

By the time Phil got there, surely enough there was a delay of a couple minutes. But still I was going in cold, stiff necked and all. I had to pretend it didn't matter. The man was my age, I later found out just a few months older than I. I knew to be aggressive. And so I was. I missed my attempted *takedown* I was lifted up, and slammed on my back with a forearm to the face.

Initially, my opponent paused, thinking he'd knocked me out. No, upon landing, I fractured my collarbone and felt all the pain of a slight dislocation of the sternal head that had sheared the soft tissues at the clavicular and sternal head areas. I had incurred a slightly separated shoulder. Then the fight started. *'No way in hell'*. I thought am I going to give into pain. *'I've rolled with bigger, more powerful men. This was only the beginning and I'd make it work.'*

After about a minute forty-five seconds, I'm slowly getting to half-guard. Phil is screaming and doing the shrimping move on the side of the ring where coaches can call out orders. And he is doing the movement, and comically to the on-looker, it looks as if Phil has a tick and can't move from his position on his side. He looks like a dyeing bug trying one last time to feel life, looking goofy enough on his side.

My opponent cannot do anything with me. I'm slowly moving out of his dominant position. I hear him breathing I can feel his heart beat. He's getting tired. I remain calm as if I have all day for this. I've had men nearly three times my weight train with me. So I am not alarmed. I know I've incurred damage, but am managing to ignore it, because Phil said, *'be aggressive and don't get submitted'*. I know I must remain active, there's always a chance for this guy to make a mistake.

Then as I begin to be more settled with half-guard and move to get full, I don't yet know how to sweep. The buzzer sounds. I know he's won the match for the take down and the mount position. He wins by four points.

We get up, we shake hands. I sure hoped Phil was happy with my performance. The guy had good weight down on me for sure. We are ordered to take our Velcro anklet bands for scoring off. He gets the win with his arm raised and wins on points.

My opponent's coach and my coach shake hands, smiling. I think, *'Hey man. This is cool I just wrestled a man in competition'.* I wanted to laugh. It is such a hilarious thought. Yet I'm so into it. It's like it didn't matter that I was a female. That's just like when I was eight years old and playing football with the boys and *'King of the Hill'* with Mike and Mark Fordham. The thrill is back.

My opponent, shakes his head with a smirk. He couldn't believe I ate the slam to the floor, and kept going. He was polite and honorable. And the cooler thing was I believe he too had been in the Marines.

The reason why years later I realized I could take such a slam and not be alarmed, was perhaps the rough-housing as a child included some brutal slams, and tackles that knocked the wind out of me. Also I knew from the age of four that no one likes a complainer. And thirdly, I had been through a vicious attack nearly twenty years before, slammed multiple times into the macadam head first by a man near 270 pounds. And I didn't die. So no reason to panic here. It's merely a chess game.

My next match was against another forty to forty-nine year old man, supposedly a beginner as well. Again he too panicked, he feared losing to me. I was about a few years his senior. The first guy wasn't a sand-bagger, the second guy I sensed was. Now looking back, you could smell it a mile away. But as usual I never saw anything as unfair.

This man was desperate to finish me. He panicked so much so that he actually started to do an illegal move. Well, for beginner it was. Not if he were in expert or advanced divisions. Phil saw it, he yelled to the referee. The referee stopped the man. It would have damaged me, perhaps permanently. At the time I was unaware of this move. That was because Phil caught the guy ready to do it. The attempt I saw later on Peter Dell 'Orto's phone video he'd shot. In the end the guy won by three points. He beat the guy who'd beaten me, I believe on points as well to get the Gold medal.

I sat in the bleachers, telling Peter, "I just took some arnica pellets. I need some ice. I'll be fine. If I can, just find my rescue concoction."

Peter now seemed in a panic. He knew I wouldn't say anything unless I thought I might be injured. But I didn't want Phil to know.

I just told him "Ahh a little sore." I made sure I could move my arm a little and look relaxed. No way was I bailing on this golden opportunity.

Soon, Peter got me an ice pack, and I stuffed it under my bra inside my shirt. The collarbone and sternal head areas hurt, the shoulder smarted. I got nailed because I was too cold. Now I was worried about the ice on my collarbone getting me to become even colder, and freezing my body taking away the warmth of the competition.

However, before my next eight matches, Phil finished up with two of our other teammates. Peter had one more to go but not for a while. Peter and Phil worked on warming me up, and keeping me warm. Because of my 105-106 weight, very low pulse, blood pressure, and low body fat I get chilled fast. I then was called for a women's match.

The three of us made our way over, to see which match was next at the ring scheduled on the program list. They'd given us a program upon us signing up and entering the arena earlier. However, now hours later and delays in the start times for certain women's divisions everything was switched around.

So we eventually figured out where to go. We saw I had about twenty minutes before the next couple matches. The next two were women's matches. I lost, but again I was not submitted by these bigger, and more experienced women. They basically just had the take down and mount, not much else did they accomplish.

I protected my collarbone, without anyone noticing, replacing smiling instead of wincing. I moved onto another women's match across the way, again the girl was more experienced, and twenty pounds heavier. Every woman I went against was not over thirty years of age. Again, I was aggressive. Remaining aggressive showed Phil, *'I was fine'*. It showed to my opponents that, I was not intimidated by youth, experience, or size. This to me was all still fun.

I lost to a third woman by points. Again, she got good position, and won on points. Then I had three men's matches. They came in a flurry. They got positioning on me. I almost got a guillotine, in two of the matches.

Yet I had a tough time maintaining the hold. These young men were just very good at positioning, and keeping their weight down.

Two of the young men in their early twenties were the closest to my size, weight, and experience. Those were the most fun matches of all. They were Novice, Bantam Weight (120-129.9 pounds). The fights were awesome. The third young man was a beginner, Bantam Weight. Again, he could only get position on me.

One of the men's coaches could not believe my strength, stamina, and the fact that I was barely breathing. I was remained relaxed, and calm during all the matches.

Unlike my opponents the one thing I noticed over and over again, was my opponent's cardio was low. Phil saw this too. Peter and Phil surmised, had the matches been longer I may have gotten the upper hand in a few of them.

My last two matches, were women's matches. I lost the first match to points, as I had the eight previous in the last three hours. Then my tenth match came. They called out my opponent's name over, and over again for minutes I waited. She was a *'no show'*. Apparently she'd left the arena. Peter, myself, and one of our other teammates went home with medals.

In the end Peter left just before Phil and I departed. Unknown to me I lost eight pounds in three hours of fighting. I now weighed ninety-eight pounds. I'm sure it was a result of the pain. But I wasn't feeling horrible till I got into my minivan.

As Phil and I collected our things, Phil looked at me and I only prayed he'd lift up my knapsack for me. Because, I didn't think I could.

As Phil was picking up gear and my knapsack he said, "I gave you an out. You never took it. I know you're injured."

I smiled, "Did anybody else know?"
Phil responded, "No. It was not noticeable."

I responded, "Okay, then good."

He said, "I only knew because I saw the slam and the way your shoulder landed, you had to be injured. And I also know you. Your movement was off in the matches afterwards. But only I would have known."

I was happy, I hid my injury well. I asked, "So how do you think I did?"

Phil responded, "Jody, you did what I told you to do. Everyone was bigger than you. You were aggressive. You always went in for the initial attack and you didn't get submitted. You did good. Real good." I was tickled pink. I couldn't wait to go home and tell Norman.

As I drove home, albeit a bit pained, I thought of what I'd accomplished and learned. I felt pretty high. I was psyched and only slightly concerned with my right arm and shoulder. I drove cautiously as to not hit too many bumps in the road driving home. I drank tons of water as

I drove. I knew the only way to speed recovery was to get well-hydrated. I was down eight pounds from the morning weigh-ins before the tournament began. I was one hundred six pounds in morning, now I weighed about ninety-eight pounds.

After I arrived home around six thirty that evening, I came in the door and said, "I'm a little pained and slight bit tired. What are you thinking dinner–wise?"

Norman replied, "How about pizza tonight. The kids want it. I'm cool with it. You had a long day. I bought beer."

I responded, "I'm a little pained. Can I have a beer? Pizza is fine. Been taking arnica pellets a couple times today."

Norman asked, "How did it go?"

I fetch a beer from the fridge, popping open the bottle I say, "Well, I *gotta* call Sue. I think I sort of fractured my collarbone. But I'm good. I have a lot of work to do tomorrow. I got the cleaning, cooking and weeding to get done. So tonight I'll rest. Phil knows I'm damaged. I just didn't tell him how much pain I'm in. Because you know, it is what it is. And I *gotta* work and do stuff anyway. And I *ain't* dead. And Good God! It was *sooo* much fun!" I laugh.

Norman asks, "So, you got medals?"

I replied, "Yes, but I was supposed to have ten matches. I had nine, the last kid, like bailed or something. She was there originally. Then they called her name over and over again and she was nowhere to be found. I really was so tired, and pained by then."

I continued, "I got injured very first match. A hundred sixty pound guy went for a *takedown* the same time I did. And of course he was stronger. That I did expect. About twenty-five seconds into this first match that happens, and then the fight starts. No way was I *gonna* let pain stop me. I've had worse. Peter did great. And get a load of this Jordan submitted the guy who I fought in the first match, his son. She won over the son. Yep. Gold medal she got it."

I took a sip of beer, "I'm going to shower now. Then I'll call Sue. See if she can see me Monday morning before work. I think Phil thinks I did okay."

The next day I got chores done and cooked meals for the week. Running fourteen miles was quite painful at first with each step. But then I just grind through it. '*I'd ran with worse and made it through races*'. I thought to myself. '*This I can do*'.

I called Sue. She called me back, and could see me the next day, Monday morning before I had to be at work, working on bodies.

Monday, soon arrived and I was in Sue's office. I figured, if I could lift my right arm and not show pain, no one would think I was any too injured. I succeeded somewhat. However, Sue checked the sternal head, acromion, and the right shoulder area.

She then said, "Hmmm anybody else would have stopped fighting, and went to the hospital. Been on pain killers and be in a sling today. Did you even take an ibuprofen?"

I responded, "No way. I used arnica cream, rescue remedy to rub and I iced the first thirty-six hours. I did take arnica pellets the first day. Then I had a beer at night when I got home."

Sue replied, "Only you." Sue shook her head, checking my thoracic and neck areas out. She continued, "You're not going to work today, are you?"

I clearly was. As I was in my whites, I said, "Hey, man I got people in pain coming in. I ain't bailing on them. This is minor." Little did Sue know I wanted to see if I could train later that night just gently drilling at Phil's. I didn't want to miss anything, learning as much as I could. And I didn't want Phil to know just how badly I felt. I also kept thinking, that Phil would think I was a wimp if I didn't even attempt to come in to try and train.

After I saw Sue, my shoulder started to get worse. By the time I got to work, just thirty minutes later after running an errand before getting to the office. I then could not lift my right arm up to ninety degrees to reset my treatment table. So I dragged the covers and sheets across the treatment table with both my hands instead of lifting my arms up. I acted as though it was normal.

This was so no one I was treating would know I was injured.

Then I had my secretary call up a local medical facility store to see if they had any undergarment collarbone braces. They did, I had her retrieve it the next day during work hours for me.

As the work day passed I got used to the pain, so long as I stayed within the range of motion of the pain. Then soon it was time to lock up and go home. Or go to Phil's. I have to say, I was very motivated to go to Phil's. I felt good about competing and about competing like the men in my gym, against men. That was really super cool to me.

I called Norman and told him I was going to venture out from the office up to Phil's Basement gym. Norman said, "Okay be careful."

I responded, "Yes, honey. I will. I'll go slow. If it doesn't feel good I'll refrain. I just *gotta* try."

We get off the phone, then I headed off to Phil's basement gym. By the time I get there I'm about twenty minutes late. It's the Monday night seven o'clock class. The place is packed. It was tough getting a parking space. I had to park on Phil's lawn. That's how it would be after a weekend of fights or tournaments. It was like everyone would get motivated that hadn't fought or grappled. We'd had about four or five guys ground fighting on Saturday in all.

So now it was the time for stories. Or so it seemed. And who would partake in the story questions, were the

ones who hadn't gone at all. Phil would tell the stories
as people warmed up. I missed all that, that night.
Earlier in the day I had seen someone Phil knew in my
office. They blabbed that I saw a doctor for my
shoulder, because they knew I had matches on Saturday
and asked me how it went. I told them.

I figured if they told Phil, he'd know already how I
was anyway, so really what did it matter? So after
parking my car, into Phil's Basement Gym I walked.
The place is packed. The gym is filled with the air of the
warmth of working bodies. There must've been fourteen
or so guys there.

As I got my clothes ready to take a walk into the
caged in room, I waited for the timer to go off. So the
guys who were fighting upon first entrance would be
stopped during their one minute rest. Then I could walk
pass them saying, 'hi', and proceeded walking over the
red matted gym floor to the bathroom to get changed.

As I did so, Phil said, "So she had to go to the doctor
and get checked. Can you believe it? So a one hundred
sixty pound guy slams her, and she's in pain. And today
she goes to the doctor."

I respond, "Well, I decided just to get checked, so I
could know what to do for myself."

I don't know it at the time, Phil, is actually being
sarcastic. The guys aren't saying anything. I felt bad. I
felt like I failed Phil's expectation of me. I really didn't
know what to say. So I reply, "I can work with my left

95

side. Right side's a little damaged." Phil is still being
funny, unknown to me.

Phil says, "Mike is injured. So work with Mike."

Mike looks at me and says, "What can you do?"

I respond, "You can use me. But just not the right
arm. I'll guard it." I thought to myself as I headed
towards the bathroom to get dressed in gym gear, *'I have
to turn off the emotional button tonight.'*

I go into the bathroom, get changed, and store my
clothing back outside of the cage entrance. Then I re-
enter the caged in gym, when the fight buzzer is again
sounded. Phil is still chatting as guys are working. Phil
is all 'up'. Peter and Jordan actually did great. I had no
clue now, at this point how I would be viewed.
'Would I be accepted?' Meanwhile I didn't know Phil
was busting me for coming in injured. So as I work with
Mike, we try not to tweak each other. I had one *'ouch'*
moment that I was not careful. The rest of the time was
all achy, dull pains.
When class was over I went into the bathroom and
changed. I actually felt better mentally. I thought to
myself, *'If Phil can't see how dedicated I am. Then
there is nothing else to show. Nothing else to do.'* So as
the guys were all leaving and saying 'good-bye', I was
putting my socks on. I was now outside the cage sitting
in one of the white plastic chairs outside of the caged in
gym.

Then with two guys in the back of the gym still doing extra '*Live*' grappling, Phil walks towards the cage door entrance. I ask, "So you're disappointed in me?"

Phil responds, "Jody, no."
I ask, "Then why did you make fun of me for going to the doctor? I had to know what to take care of on my body. I wasn't going to give up. You know I'm not stupid. And I really am injured."

Phil says, "Jody, I'm making fun of you, because what person do you know screws up their shoulder and knows they are damaged and keeps going? No. Not just through that match but to the very end, like ten matches. I gave you an out. You didn't take it. I knew you were injured. You had to be. But you acted as though nothing happened. You kept going. Everyone was bigger than you."

I replied, "So you mean, you knew how injured I was? I knew you knew I was somewhat injured. But I didn't want to complain. But I had to be smart."

Phil says, "Yes. Also the guys I know. They just fight and they are not back in here after a tournament or fight usually for the whole week. And they are not even really injured. Here you are, injured after a tournament and you're back in here. People don't usually do that."

I reply, "Oh. So you don't think I'm a wimp. Huh?"

Phil responded, "No. Jody, you made me proud. You did everything I told you to do. You didn't complain, and you were really injured."

I asked, "How did you know I was injured? I was trying to hide it."

Phil replied, "That slam was bad. You had to be injured. No way could you not have been injured. I saw how you landed on your shoulder. Even the guy you were fighting thought he knocked you out, and then you're going for a submission with your damaged side right after that. I saw him stop, lift up and check you. And besides I know you. I did not expect you to come in tonight. No one else would have."

I felt a sense of relief. I asked, "So the guys weren't thinking I wasn't worth working with? Like they knew you were cajoling me?"

Phil replied, "Yes. I let them know how tough you are. And they know how you did. My wife yelled at me for letting you to continue, after I knew you were injured."

I replied, "That's crazy. She doesn't know fighting. Thank God she wasn't there."

After we chatted a bit, I said 'good-bye' and drove home. I couldn't wait to put my rub on the injury and lay down strapping my arm in close to my body for the night.

Undomesticated…

She's undomesticated so they say,
And with the boys she did play.
Her Mom expressed to her dismay,
This playing with boys will end some day.

One summer eve an alarm was rang,
Her mother thought her chest had sprang.
The sadness she felt,
Was a bump not welt.

Her Mom called the doctor.
He told her to explore,
The possibilities of her,
Becoming woman forever more.

Her Mom did check,
It seemed to be,
That a woman
Was to grow inside of she.

The undomesticated one you see,
Is not what everyone else thought she'd be.
Their wants and desires
She would not fulfill.
Because it lacked her desired thrill.

Chapter Fourteen
We Call Him Joe
Thursday July 30th, 2009

It was now nearly five weeks since the tournament and I was getting ready for the next tournament, which was on August 1st in two days. I was back to somewhat normal training seventeen days after. The pain had subsided greatly after two and a half weeks.

However, this Thursday morning eleven thirty class, only Joe and I were the ones who showed up for class that morning. I'd hardly worked with this young Middle-eastern twenty-something year old man. He was painfully shy, quiet, very slender, and tall. Joe, appeared kind, bashful and had an essence of trepidation. His cousin Felix was a very kind, and considerate successful man of Syrian descent. Felix was hard-working, and so too was Joe. Although I don't think 'Joe' was his real first name. He easily was referred to by that name.

So after we got dressed in our training attire, Phil says, "Let's work stand up."

I respond, "Sure, I'd love to."

Joe responds with almost no words. I see much trepidation. I say, "Hey, I'm new at this aspect. We will go light. Besides I have NAGA tournament on Saturday. I'm cool with it."

Joe has this blank expression on his face. He is a bit afraid. So I thought, '*is he afraid of hurting me?*' Then

I realized, 'he would've said something to Phil if he were.'

Then I said, "Hey if you're afraid of getting punched in the face. You know I'd rather get punched in the face then get a manicure."

Phil then chimes in reading what I'm getting at and says, "I'd rather get punched in the face then rake leaves."

I say, "Oh, Yeah, I'd rather get punched in the face than go to a beauty salon."

Phil says, "I'd rather get punched in the face than shovel snow."

Upping the anti I say, "Well, I'd rather get punched in the face than shop for a dress."

Phil says, "Joe it's not so bad." Okay so Phil now realizes Joe and I are going to spar. And I'm thinking, *'this guy is over six feet tall. I'd better cover up and get in close'.* But yet, I don't want to look like a wimp. But I know I would rather fight than get my nails done. Now that would just be torture.
We get shin guards and gloves on. And as we begin to go at it. I realize Joe is less proficient than I am at sparring. He is running away from me. So then Phil stops us. Phil says, "This is a Jody. Not a woman. It's okay. She's okay with getting hit."

Joe and I begin again to spar. It was great. He really adjusted well and we got good sparring in. And we sort of kind of became good gym buddies. So much so that one day when one of the older guys in the gym who was being a bit of a jerk, told Joe to put his hands down so he punch him in the face when they were doing a drill. Joe innocently complied. I found out. I was fuming, "Phil, give me that guy. That's just wrong. I'll teach him." I made certain Joe wasn't there to hear me. But Joe to me was young enough to be my son. He was sweet, kind, and a hard-working guy. I can respect that always.

Then one day, Joe blossomed. He had matured now into his mid-twenties it had seemed. And man, could he kick. He gained confidence over the next year or so. He improved so much, I could no longer hold Muay Thai pads for as long a time for him as I had been able to for the head kicks he threw. They were just awesome. The power and speed were ridiculous. He now could spar with almost anyone in the gym. Phil's Basement Gym is what this young man needed. And it was wonderful to see him achieve it.

Chapter Fifteen
I survived August 1ˢᵗ 2009

In my third Grappling Tournament ever on August 1, 2009, my coach Phil Dunlap and I signed me up again for multiple divisions, levels, and weight classes as we had in the last grappling tournament. This tournament was called "The Battle at the Beach," a NAGA event.

At the time there were women's divisions, yet no one was near my weight class in the women's divisions. The men's divisions had lighter weight classes at the Novice and Beginner levels. We were trying to get me as many matches as possible.

There in a tournament, in a realm I just entered. It is where only the young, mostly men, bigger people than I who were more experienced competed for their prizes. Phil and I also wanted to see what I could handle, and where I was at. I'd pretty much been training with all men who were 130-280 lbs in Phil's Fight Gym. I fattened up to 106lbs that morning before weighing in.

I was a novice, I started in February 2009 learning ground work for the first time. My wrestling experience was that I had a Native American friend in high school, Joanne Yelloweyes.

Joanne had given me three hours of her time one week when she was in from college. I was sixteen. It was December 1978. She was willing to teach me boys wrestling, and the self-defense she'd learned at Rutgers.

My other experience was my husband Norman gave me a chance to do *Budokai Karate* and I took a few lessons in the summer of 1985. But I just didn't dig the whole belt, *gi*, and bowing thing. I loved the wrestling Joanne taught me, and I loved the idea of boxing. My sport watching had been mostly of the NFL and Boxing, since 1966/67. So I was indeed a Novice.

Again, since the men had the lightest weight class available at Novice and Beginner in the weight classes closest to mine. Phil and I signed me up for Men's open (eighteen and up); Bantam Weight (120-129.9 pounds) Novice (zero to six months experience) and Beginner (zero to eighteen months experience). We then signed me up for the Women's Open (eighteen and up), beginner 130-139.9 pounds weight class. Then we signed me up for the women's over forty, intermediate (two to five years experience) division, 130-139.9 pounds. Then we signed me up for the Women's thirty to thirty-nine, Advanced/Expert Division, 130-139.9 pounds.

I was happy; just five weeks prior at a Grappler's Quest Tournament I had five divisions, nine ground fights, five men and four women. I knew the experience would help me get closer to my goals.

I might not win these ground fights. But I didn't care about winning. I wanted to experience the process of learning.

The way many of these tournaments work, is there are usually four levels: Novice, Beginner, Intermediate, and Advanced/Expert.. Then there are age groups in adults like so: eighteen and up (Open), thirty to thirty-nine years of age, forty to forty-nine years of age, fifty- to fifty-nine years of age, and age sixty and over.

Then there are weight classes, usually with some exceptions but usually a range of ten pound weight classes like so: 119.9lbs and under, 120-129.9lbs, 130-139.9 lbs, etc...

There are usually eleven to thirteen circles at the event. So there can be as many as thirteen fights going on at the same time. The referees, along with cooperation of the fighters, are to stay in their outlined circles in their assigned areas on medium soft mats. Similar to wrestling mats.

You win or lose usually under 'normal' circumstances by submission or points due to a take down, positioning, and/or attempted submissions. It has an air of wrestling to it, yet many good positions in grappling are not desired in wrestling. And there are really no points for pinning your opponent in grappling, unlike wrestling. Grappling can be much rougher than wrestling.

So here I was ready to have maybe ten ground matches of all different levels. When I got called over to the Men's, Bantam 120-129.9 pound weight-class, beginner division, ages eighteen and up. Most of the men were in their twenties.

Two from the last tournament recognized me. One young twenty-two year old man I'd grappled with at the Grappler's Quest five weeks earlier smiled and said, "Hey, come here. Sit with us." He motioned to me, then continued, "This is the lady that I fought and I told you guys about. She's my Mom's age." Two of the young men smiled, shook my hand, and welcomed me to sit down with them as our names were called to be paired up to fight in the first round.

The tournament was so big and that division was so packed. There must have been twenty guys. I lost my first match on points. But I was aggressive. Then minutes later, I was called to another area of mats for another division. I wrestled an expert woman who was in her late thirties. She seemed nice. I got the *takedown*. I couldn't believe it. It was my first good *takedown* in a competition. This lady was really well known and was an expert to boot.

However, I lost on points. The positioning of my body to be able to take advantage of my *takedown* was diminished by her athleticism and her expertise. Then I got called back to the men's open division, novice category, bantam weight again. And again I lost on points. However, I was aggressive as Phil had wanted. He again said, "I'm looking for aggression from you, and do not get submitted."

I understood and maintained both those two thoughts throughout the day of grappling. However, I wondered, 'when was I going to submit an opponent. Here I was in my third tournament and I still hadn't submitted any one of my opponents.

Then I was called over to the women's mat area again, same corner different division, weight class and category. The woman was early thirties, tall, weighed about 130 pounds and was an intermediate grappler. Phil pointing said, "That's your opponent. Snatch that head down, and guillotine her."

I replied, "Okay. You sure that's the one? I see that long beautiful neck. Yes, good target."

Phil repeats, "Snatch her head down, and guillotine her. She won't be able to get out of your guillotine."

106

They call our names and sure enough Phil is correct who my opponent is. The referee introduces us, we shake hands. He says, "Timers ready? Go."
  I see fear in her eyes as I move in. She comes in hesitantly. I get her. I grab and snatch the head down under my left armpit. She's tapping. I won. After they announce that I've won, and gave me a medal. I step off the mat, I look at Phil I start to lose it. Phil grabs me. Holds me I can't believe I'm crying. He pulls me over. I keep saying, "I can't believe I won. I can't believe I won. I really won. I can't believe it."

Phil responds, "You did great."

I respond, "I'm sorry I got upset. But I'll tell you later what today is. It's something."

  I get called again and go against a woman in the intermediate division who's in her late thirties and weighs in the 140-149.9 pound weight class, I lose to points.
  Then I fight another young man in the open division, beginner, bantam-weight class, I lose to him on points. Phil and I wait to see if I get called again for the men's open division, novice bantam-weight class again. I missed a match there due to the fact I was competing in another area at the same time against one of the women. So after that I am done for the day.
  Phil, is watching other matches as I wander around speaking to some of the men and women who I've fought against and some who realize my age and small size and want to talk to me. Kyle O. has finished

competing and I'm working on his back again in between all this.

I drank some water, as I calmed, alone in my thoughts. I start watching the Women's Absolute division. And who do I see? Tara LaRosa. I was in awe of watching her get out of submission attempts by bigger women in the Absolute matches. I can't remember what it was, but we ended up facing each other after I was finished and she had just finished a match. We began to talk.

I saw her reach and grab her neck after winning a match that she looked like she just might not get out of this wicked submission attempt. I hesitated at first, but then my care-giving side couldn't help myself. I asked, "Hey uh. Are you okay? I'm an ART practitioner. You alright?"

Tara LaRosa responds rubbing her neck, "Yeah. Just a little cranked."

I ask, "You going to be alright for your next match? I'd like to see you take it."

Tara says, "Thanks. I think I'm good." She stands on one side of the blocked fenced off competitor area and I'm now done competing standing on the other side, by the spectator area.

I ask, "So how in the world did you get out of that, looked like a full-nelson? That was so impressive."

Tara responds making up a funny name. I later tried to repeat it to Phil. Yet, as I did I started to laugh and forgot it. She said, "I just made it up." She chuckled.

We chatted a little more, then she was called to her next match, I wish her well. As she went to compete in her next match, I recognized something. Her right ear was cauliflower, my left ear was cauliflower. Her left collarbone looked a little off, like it had been damaged. I knew my right collarbone was damaged five weeks prior. I thought, '*how funny*'.

As I watched matches, I then hear my name being called. It's Phil he's ready to leave. I'm tired and I have nearly a three hour drive back home as does Phil. Phil says, "You ready to go?"

I reply, "Yeah. I got something to tell you outside."

As we pick up our items, and walk out through the Wildwood Convention Center, where the tournament took place. Saying '*good-bye*' to people on our way. We get to my car and I say, "Phil, guess what today is?"

Phil, looks at me, "What?"

I answer, "I was worried, that I'd be preoccupied mentally today. I wondered, 'how would I overcome it?' How could I forget, when I am reminded every day of my life what today is since August 1st, 1991? I survived. Today is the eighteenth anniversary of the attack on me that I should've been dead. You know. You don't just forget stuff like that."

Phil responded, "Wow. That's big Jody."

I continued, "So I wonder why I lost it and cried when I won. And then it dawned on me. I've won in many ways."

We said our good-byes. I told Phil, "Call me when you guys get home. Let me know you're safe. Thanks again Phil."

Fear Not

Feign the evidence of the fear.
Endless lies with no tear.
Already carrying haunted blame.
Random thoughts mislead the lame.
No one ever threatens test.
Oblivious to their growth in spirit.
Tortured fear douses the lit.

Jody-Lynn Reicher

Chapter Sixteen
"Fighting is Like Volleyball, Only a Little Closer... (August 15th, 2009)"

In Phil's basement gym on August 15th, 2009, Friday group MMA (Mixed Martial Arts) training began. Phil always has this air about him, and his teaching that went something like this, "Okay, you up or down?" The men would respond in kind. Then Phil would pair each one up based on up or down. Up, meaning stand-up work. Such as punches, kicks, and knees, and possible sparring. That depended on each person's choice. Down meant, wrestling, grappling, working on technical ground moves and what we call *'going Live'*.

Funny enough, it didn't matter what size you were. If someone was 240 pounds and was *up,* and you were 145 pounds and you wanted *up.* Then, that's what it was. It was *'up'.* Well till you got knocked out, broken, you quit or it was end of session.

Ninety-five percent of the men were fair. Ninety percent had quite a bit of self-control. Phil demanded it. He never really said it. It may have just been the way he walked, in front of you. And there's a feeling of, *'let's just be fair'.*

However, if you lacked self-control, well there were consequences. Not something we talked about, because it really rarely happened. There was no complaining, it just all worked itself out.

This particular night I came in, not knowing what Phil had planned on me to do. I just had finished my third grappling tournament, and I was leaving for vacation the next day. I'd be away for a week. I needed hard training just to feel alive, and keep that feeling inside as I was on vacation.

Since March I'd been getting ready to become a MMA fighter. I wanted to get a good sweat, and a really good training set in that night. It was seven o'clock, and time to begin. Adam, Peter, Scott, and I had just shown up inside Phil's basement gym. I looked and wondered, *'who will do what?'*

I was familiar with all the men. Scott, known as 'The Cloud', his weight range was between 215-240 pounds and standing six feet five inches tall. Scott had played some football in college before going further into pre-med education. Scott came from a line of surgeons.

Peter, had a high IQ. Peter was of Northern Italian and Polish descent. Peter fought in Japan. He was an ESL (English as a Second Language) Teacher. He also was a translator. He understood computers so well that he'd written and published many PDF files. Peter did Personal Training on the side for extra money. He understood the human body fairly well. Peter, still in his thirties stood six feet four inches tall, and weighed about 185 pounds.

Then there was Adam who was of Polish and Japanese descent. He was in his early thirties. Adam stood about five feet nine inches tall, and weighing in at about 165 pounds. Adam was a well-educated, and a very quiet man. He was probably one of the most responsible young men I'd ever met, along with the other two men that were there that night as well. Adam's manners were impeccable. He was super kind, and caring. Probably the nicest guy you'd ever meet.

So here we were by seven o'clock, the four of us with Phil. Phil asked, "You up, or down." Peter and Scott were *'down'*. Adam was flexible. Phil put up the rope at the front of the caged in section. He wanted Adam, and I to spar. I'd done very little sparring up until that point.

Adam was technically skilled, it seemed in everything. I wanted to do stand-up for certain. Phil wanted me to do it too. Adam was smooth and flowing on the ground, it seemed he had a former wrestling background. At this point I'd never seen Adam do any stand-up.

I started with a little stand-up in July. I assumed Adam would strike, and flow just as well in stand-up as he did on the ground. I'd already experienced his flow on the ground. So in the beginning of our stand-up Adam was smooth and elusive.

Then I began to be able to chase him down, he barely struck me, and not really completely punch me back. I was at first perplexed. Finally, I realized Adam was being kind. He probably was taught not to hit a girl. Phil realizing this said, "Adam, go work with Scott and Peter."

Phil, goes to the bin to get a pair of four ounce gloves. Phil is going to spar with me. Adam seeing this says, "Oh no."

Phil then sets up the timer. After he does he gets a sip of water, and putting on a pair of four ounce gloves says, "Okay we'll do three, five minute professional rounds." I look at Phil and wonder, *'which way do I go?'*

Before I know it, as to my nature I move forward. Knowing that you're going to get hit and getting hit are two different things. It is scarier to know you're going to get hit than it is to get hit. Getting hit is nothing. It's the fear leading up to it. That's the torture. Once the blow lands, nothing else matters anymore. You're either in the fight or you're done.

Phil is throwing punches and kicks. He's not airing it out. Yet, I am fighting for my life. Soon the first round buzzer sounds. I notice nothing but the angle I must try to take and to keep my hands up. I am focused only on those tasks at hand.

The second round buzzer sounds. We begin again. I wonder how I'm doing. '*Am I brave enough to follow through all three rounds with Phil?*' That question is always with me. As Phil punches and kicks me, I try taking him down. Time passes. I stand up after failing to take Phil down. Because if I don't he will just drag me with his foot and leg and I'm then nowhere. And I'm not tired. I want to show Phil that I'd prefer to stand, when I fight.

As we spar I hear, "Com'on Jodes..." The three men, Adam, Peter, and Scott in the gym have stopped their training. It's like a fight broke out or something. Scott's yelling to encourage me. Soon the other two, Adam and Peter are adding to the entourage of encouragement. The buzzer sounds. I'm now tired. The kicks and punches to the legs and body are draining.

Scott, Peter, and Adam are now focused on giving me encouragement. Phil says, "You're doing good. Last round." As much as I feel things swelling. I know I'm totally fine. This is scary and exciting all at once. It is quite freeing.

After thirty seconds of the one minute rest. I feel a little better. Then before I can ponder, the third round begins. I'm figuring, *'what tactically would be the smartest direction to get a shot in?'* The only thing I really know is to keep my hands up and to be aggressive. It's the mantra now playing inside my head.

As we go at it again for a third round, I can hear the guys coaching me. I'm groping, trying to stay on my feet. As I try to keep my forward motion going. I go in for another take down attempt. I hang onto Phil's leg and foot. His balance is ridiculous. Every time I'd go to grab the other leg, my shoulders, arms, and head would get punched. I finally hang on to the takedown attempt, and succeed.

I had imagined Phil seeing me work hard for the take down, and probably let me get hold of the other leg. The worst part of my take down came when he just rolled me over and into his dominant position. Phil was crushing me as he'd done many times before prepping me to compete in grappling tournaments against men. It was to see how far I could be pushed.

Phil would say then and in the future, "Be aggressive. I want aggression and don't get submitted. Those are your goals". Those were easy orders to take. I was driven to never disappoint Phil, or the men who worked with me. As always, I desire to win for my coach, my team, my family and then for me.

Soon enough the third round buzzer sounded. Phil taking off his gloves says, "Good work." The guys are high-fiving me and whooping it up. My body started to shake. I needed part of a protein bar to continue to train. Phil wanted me to work ground with Scott next.

As we worked ground technique, Marcus came in late bringing his son Tyson in. They missed all the fun. The next time Marcus would see Phil take me to task would be ten days later. And it so would blow his mind.

Figure 2. Phil's Basement Gym Ground Time

To train a Fighter.

How to train a fighter,
Is not exactly clear.
There's no particular righter,
Way to turn their gears.

A trainer must employ themselves,
To find each fighters place.
The trainers job a selfless one,
Every fighter has a pace.

As the fighter receives their training,
Some look on with disgust.
But those who do the reining,
They know its do or bust.

The training should be harder,
Than the fight that is at hand.
For if the trainer doesn't push,
Their fighter can't take a stand.

To climb into a cage or ring,
The trainer knows what's best.
So long as fighting is their thing,
Their selfless trainer never rests.

Chapter Seventeen
"She Has a Special Talent"
(August 25th, 2009)

"You punch her in the face, she attacks you." Phil said to Keith, a man Phil had trained since 1995 who'd never competed in anything as far as we all knew. Yet, was well-trained by Phil. They were tight. However, they thought differently.

Keith saw me as an old woman. I realized this night I challenged his thinking of what a woman could be. Keith was married, he was not a kid. Albeit, he was about ten years my junior. Keith just couldn't get passed my desire to become a fighter. He appeared a bit squeamish about sparring with me. But I never realized it, till that night.

When Phil put us together in the front of the room, he instructed Keith to do pad work with me. Keith was not digging it. And I didn't know that Keith didn't seem interested in my becoming a fighter. And he appeared to not know what to really do with me. Which was confusing to me. I thought he knew most of what Phil knew. However, I was an anomaly.

Time passed in the class, and I was getting bored. I know I just had a vacation. However, even on vacation, I stay in shape. I had done drills so I wouldn't lose anything Phil had instructed me on.

Phil saw the look in my face and what Keith was doing with me. Keith did not want to '*move*' with me. Albeit the place was packed, yet Phil had set up the rope so when Keith decided to have me spar with him, then everything was already set up for us. I knew Keith would be brutal. Only because that was just the way Phil worked it in his gym. I was one of the guys. I was to become a fighter as I wished, yet sparring with different guys with different styles was the best way to see where your flaws were.

Before I knew it, class was ending and even though the gym was packed, it seemed as though no one wanted to *roll* extra with Phil. Again, there were at least fifteen guys in that night. So it was odd that no one wanted to *roll* with Phil at the end of that night's session.

Then Phil announced, "That'll be a session. Anybody want to *roll* with me, let me know." Everyone stopped. He looked at me. I was itching to spar. Phil asked, "You want to *move*?"

I responded, "Yeah."

Phil said, "Okay." He walked over to a bin with four ounce gloves and shin guards in it and donned the attire. I was already wearing shin pads, four ounce gloves and my mouth guard.

I can't remember if Phil even set the timer. I didn't care. I was itching to see where I was at. Always having a bit of trepidation, yet I needed to know, *was I a fighter*?

There was barely a moment that I thought I was a female. I thought I was a person training and trying out to become a fighter in Phil's basement gym.

Then Phil asked, "You ready?"

I responded, "Yes."

Then we began. A couple guys were grappling in the back of the gym. The rest of the guys some were watching. I really wasn't paying attention. I was paying attention to the task at hand. I had said my prayers, and as I talked to St. Michael under my breath, I focused on blocking, taking angles, and trying to be aggressive enough to engage in striking Phil.

He kicked me and punched me. I attempted punching as well. I had no kicks at all at this point. It wasn't in my repertoire, and we didn't know when it would ever enter. I attempted to get into his space and attack the body, either with tight short punches or knees. Phil of course the expert as always, inhibited my strikes. Some were parried and then I was punched in the face and I kept moving forward.

My will has always been, to keep moving forward. I kept reminding myself, *'I don't retreat. Show no fear. Just move forward. You will get hit anyway. It's part of the game.'* Now I know many men were watching, they wanted to see my reaction, perhaps. They wanted to see if I'd quit. I thought, *'damn anybody who thinks I'm going quit in front of anyone let alone these tough men.'*

I've met tough men. My mind went back to the football games I played with the boys and my brother. Some wanted to hurt me to get me out of the game, like *'I'll show her.'* Or some men, who thought they were tough. And I found them to be bullies. I don't know how that happens. But it does. My Mom use to say to me about my Dad, "He's so arrogant sometimes. Don wants what Don wants." But yet not allowing my Mom to do anything she wanted to do, like work part-time.

That too, went through my mind. And as it did, I became more indignant. It pushed me to want to show these men, *that I may bleed, I may toil, but you will have to kill me to stop me. I'm not going down. I'm not going to fold. If I can move, but can't stand, I'll crawl. I will drag my body just show God, and everyone that this is what I'm meant for. Right here, right now.* This is the proving ground for me.

I can't remember exactly how long we went. However, no one seemingly wanted to roll with Phil before or after this. It could've been the hot, humid summer night air. And also, that there wasn't any air-conditioning. The place was packed which brought the temperature in the basement gym to an even higher level. That if you were not warm-weather-friendly. You weren't enthused to do more than the class session that you did.

As I look back now on that day over seven years ago, I remember I didn't know I had blood all over my face and shirt. I wore black short tights and the Asylum Black Board shorts, with my white t-shirt that had red lettering on it saying, "*Injured Marine Semper Fi Fund…*"

It was a shirt my husband had made. It's purpose was to raise awareness, and money for that charity in four of the runs I performed, mostly, invented and directed as an ultra-runner. That shirt after we finished was bloody along with my face. Nothing was broken.

Phil had landed well, when I hadn't covered up or blocked properly. I saw it as part of my learning.

We finished, Phil said, "You did good."

I responded, "Thank you." As I plopped my taxed body down in one of the white plastic chairs just outside the cage. Outside from where we were sparring. Then came the criticism. No, it was not from Phil.

As I partially rested, then took off the gloves, hand wraps, and shin guards, Marcus said, "If I was your husband I'd take a gun and shoot Phil."

I looked out at the men in the gym and the gym. I looked at Marcus and said, "I'm fine. My husband gave me his blessing to do this. I don't see the problem."

Marcus countered shaking his head, "Man…." He repeated himself. Then one of the other men, who'd done an amateur MMA event about a couple years ago, yet he'd really had not fought much under Phil's tutelage, looked at me and said, "You're disgusting."

I looked back, shrugged and said, "I'm sorry for you." And in my mind I thought, '*His poor woman. I have gone and unmanned this man too.*' He got his things and put his shoes on and left.

Keith commented to Phil. He was uncertain. Keith was married to a different type of woman. His wife was lady-like, very soft, and tender. Keith was seeing something he'd perhaps probably never witnessed in a woman.

Some didn't say anything. The fighters Phil had, remained. A few didn't understand. However, the guys who were real fighters understood, and they remained.

As the time passed that night, and the following days, the men who could respect the fact that Phil would treat me as an equal were fine with it. He would treat anyone who wanted to be a fighter under his tutelage, with equality and this I knew.

In doing so, Phil could now see who his fighters were. Albeit this new transition, was not easy. A few people were harder more on Phil than I, or any of the other guys in the gym at this point. There were some nice compliments. So I didn't notice any other negatives coming from any other guys. It was like a mixed review on a car in a *JD Powers* consumer report.

I found this out on the next night, a Wednesday at nine o'clock. It was in my private lesson with Phil, that a few of the guys came down hard on him. I told Phil, "You know. I now know who the real fighters are in here. I know what a real man is. And the ones who remarked inappropriately, have too much ego in here. They are the same type of people that I found of the women who made snide remarks when I was doing self-defense. They are little people with small minds and I don't need them. And it appears, I've unmanned some of the men. Well tough."

I knew inside myself, the men who were not saying anything had to either think about it. Or they thought, '*good test.*' I soon found out, that over the next month there were only a few who couldn't handle it. Most appeared willing to accept me fighting. They realized I was not forced to fight or spar with Phil that night.

Yet, but to the contrary, that I was more than willing. And that I knew what it was going to take to become a fighter under Phil's tutelage. I knew what Phil expected.

This would not be the first or the last time I would spar Phil in front of the men in the gym. As a matter of fact, Phil saw that I desired a test like this from him sort of regularly.

Also that, once the men saw me sparring Phil more often, they didn't have a problem giving me their best majority of the time when they had to spar me. It also encouraged them to spar and roll with Phil, when they perhaps were hesitant to do so in the past.

I also knew that for me this was just like being in the Marines, playing football with my brother and his buddies when I was a kid. It had a similar feel to it. I know I had to show my willingness to spar with anyone, no matter how sacred I might be of them. And Phil is always scary. Yet, I decided that it was great preparation for lowering my anxiety when it came to the time that we took a real fight for me.

No matter how it would all turn out, Phil let me know I was actually doing as much as I could in training and being consistent. Those are some of the things that are pertinent to being a fighter. Your coach has to believe in you enough to stick his neck out for you, and get you those fights. Regardless, of what others say.

Two days later, there would be a slight delay in our sparring sessions. I was sparring a young man, six foot one inch tall and lanky 168 pounds. I ducked under his punches and coming up for an upper cut, I cleared my face too soon and he nailed my left eye socket.

Brendan and Phil saw it. It was the first time they'd seen me backup slightly. I was a little disoriented, I saw three Justin's out of my left eye, one Justin out of my right eye. I actually knew I was injured, but thought 'no way is it that bad'. Brendan said, "Stop! Phil!"

Phil said, "You need to stop Jody."

Justin and I stopped. I responded, "I think I'm okay."

Phil said, "No you took a good shot." Then that's when I saw three of one person out of my left eye.

Then I said, "Uh oh. I see three Hiam's out of my left eye. Phil, what the *hec*? I feel okay otherwise."

Phil said, "It may clear. Just do pad work."

Soon, it cleared in twenty minutes. The sight was the same in both eyes and fine. No real pain, but a bit bruised, so it felt. As I held pads for Justin, he said, "My Mom thinks this fighting is stupid."

I ask, "Yeah, well she's your Mom. What does your Dad think?"

Justin says, "He's cool with it. He does think it's good."

I reply, "Well, he's right. You're going to go away for college and I'd want my kid to be well-trained, boy

127

or girl. You don't know what's out there. So it ain't stupid."

Before we knew it session was over. We all gathered our things and departed from Phil's basement gym chatting. I was the last one to exit Phil's driveway. I had a dental appointment before retrieving our children from school that afternoon. About a quarter mile down the road, I decided to wipe my nose as I drove, I had just sneezed. I went to wipe, I blew my nose, and I realized I had a left orbital blowout. Or so I thought.

I decided to turn the minivan around and get Phil's opinion. So I soon returned to Phil's home and rang the doorbell. The door opens and there's Phil. "Jody?"

I respond, "I think I have a little problem. I need your opinion. Watch what happens when I blow my nose." I blow my nose, the eyeball feels like it's rolling around.

Phil remarks, "*Oooh* that's not good. Looks like an orbital blowout."

I ask, "What do I do now?"

Phil said, "Can you see a doctor today?"

I reply, "Well, I'm going to see my dentist I've known for over twenty years. I'm seeing him for a cleaning. Should I show him?"

Phil said, "Yeah. He may have an idea."

I reply, "I'll find out who I should see from him."

Phil remarked, "Yes, that's a good idea."

So off I went to my dental appointment. However, I decided to pick up an ice cold drink to drink and then hold to my left eye at each stop light. I did this on my way to the dentist. I figured it couldn't hurt.

Soon I arrived at my dentist's office and told him what happened. He said, "You look good. However, do you have an ENT doctor?"

I responded, "Why, yes I do. I've used Dr. Harry Katz."

The dentist replied, "Give him a call."

After the dentist, and picking up our children I called the ENT's office. They got me in pretty quickly. Within days, I had a CT Scan ordered by my internist, and also I had two eye exams as well. The eye was fine. Yet, I did have an orbital blowout.

Well, the one eye doctor wanted to have me see a person he deemed an orbital surgical specialist. However, you had to foot the entire bill for the visit and the surgery, upfront. I thought, '*What the hec?*' And I found out he would only work with two orbital surgeons.

I looked into the second orbital surgeon he would work with. Yet, the ophthalmologist hadn't recommend that one first. I had to call the ophthalmologist's office to get the second name. The second one he was willing to do the surgery with, and that orbital surgeon took my insurance as well.

I later found out in all my research and calling doctors I knew from my own business, that the guy that took my insurance, really was the *go to guy* for someone like me. The other guy was for *ehhh hmmmm…Christy Brinkley* types with money. He was more of a plastic surgeon.

I then went through more eye exams, and saw the orbital surgeon. I'd also found out he was someone who had treated quite a number of Russian Fighters from Brighton Beach.

He examined my scan and my eyes for forty-five minutes. This was the sixth doctor to see my scan and my fourth exam by a doctor. He really took his time with me. So I wondered what he thought. He was a specialist and came highly-recommended, by other doctors I knew. He was in New Jersey and in Manhattan as well.

He said, "Well, I have to ask you a favor."

I responded, "Yes?"

He responded, "Your scan. Well, this is exciting. I have to show you what I found. First, I 'm a professor at Manhattan Eye and Ear."

I wondered, "Yeah? Wow! I didn't know that."

Pointing at my scan. He continued, "So you see this fracture here?"

I replied, "Oh yeah."

He then explains, "You see I've been talking about how the orbit can break away at this very section of bone during an orbital blowout. It was a theory. Now your scan is proof. Because, it's the first time I've ever seen this, and now this is proof that my theory is correct."

I responded, "Oh Wow! That's fascinating."

The surgeon continues, "So I was wondering, may I have a copy of your scan and show it to my class?"

I replied, "Well of course. If that helps people to better understand the medicine they are studying. I'm all for it."

He responds, "Thank you."

I then ask, "So are you going to do surgery on me?" Hoping the answer is I'm fine and 'no'.

He replies, "Oh no. Your eye is healthy. That's not necessary. Your body did exactly what it was intended to do. How long ago did this happen again?"

I respond, "Two weeks and a day ago."

He replies, "Two more weeks then you can fight again."

And I gave a sigh of relief.

Chapter Eighteen
A Rib Replacement (2009)

As Phil was getting me ready for another grappling tournament, I was working way too much and trying to have both our children's birthday parties as separate. Other years I'd collage them together. Now the children were getting older and I wanted them to experience their own celebrations.

I was training twenty-four to thirty hours a week and working full time. With barely any sleep and being inside for much training, which most of my years of training for athletics were spent primarily out doors.

Outside where I faced weather conditions, I was feeling a bit relieved that I was no longer doing forty to seventy-five mile runs at one in the morning. However, I was so busy I wasn't getting much sleep, which this pattern had been occurring since 2003. So far I'd survived.

Then one day in November 2009, I got the Swine Flu. Losing eight pounds in three days, while laying in bed took its toll on me. Our internist was called by Norman as I lay in bed with a near 104 fever, unable to open my eyes going into a second day. The doctor made me take ibuprofen, which I was not used to taking anything since 2003, six years plus prior to this illness.

Our internist also prescribed a quinolone antibiotic prophylactic and a flu reducer. I had a reaction to both which affected me so much, it crippled my muscles for nearly three weeks after I'd gotten better. Whatever other damage it had done I'd find out later.

About a month passed after being off the antibiotics, which I was on for four days per my doctor's orders. We figured four weeks was a good stretch to make certain I would not be susceptible to having any tendon or muscle damage from sparring, especially with Phil.

So one night for my private Wednesday lesson, Phil wanting to check where my MMA skills were now, he asked, "Do you want to *move*? You seemed warmed up."

I replied, "Yeah, sure. Just get me a little more warmed up." I had no trepidation. I felt fine.

As we spar, I'm feeling a little rusty, yet getting into my normal flow, and then getting the expected disruptions to my body from Phil's kicks, and punches to my body. I had to reset, as he would mix up his footwork.

Phil did this to wear me down. He found that the guys got tired from him feigning false moves. He wanted to make certain the fighter would keep their structure even under trickery and duress. Keeping your hands up, being able to read when to block punches and kicks to the body, legs or head, was essential.

I'd already taken a size fourteen foot to the face earlier in that autumn, via a head kick from Phil. The kind that didn't exactly ring your bell, though it could. But when you have a little sinus issue going on, the one ear fills with fluid, and you hear a whoosh...sound after the kick to the head. Then you feel like you want to pop your ears. So I would try and yawn away that whoosh between my ears or in one ear. Sometimes it last more than a day after. Phil would see me in the gym, trying to yawn. I remember saying to Phil, "It's like I got water in my ear. Hold on a second." And then I'd jump up and down on one leg like I was getting rid of potential *swimmer's ear*.

It was about mid-summer when Phil would have me spar with him. There would be no timer or bell. We would just get me warmed up and *move*. We did as much as an hour once. Usually it was thirty to forty minutes straight or until 'The Jody', couldn't pick her arms up and punch him, when I was in his guard and he'd be heel kicking my legs and hips. I would do my best not to allow too much punishment, yet I am a little stubborn.

So this one night in December, Phil is taking me to task to see where I'm at on the whole MMA fight realm. We were twenty minutes into our non-stop sparring session. Phil threw a kick to the left side of my body. Minutes later I was on the ground, after he had kicked my legs over and over again. I thought, '*I'm just not use to it*'. It had been six weeks since we sparred.

I go to get up from the matted floor. I discover I can't without some nasty left side rib pain. I look up at Phil and then drop my head and hands to the mat, "I'm trying. I can't get up. I'm really trying. What's going on?" I go to get up and I can't unfold my body.

Phil asks, "What is it?"

I reply, "My left side. My ribs."

Phil goes over to my left side, quickly lifts up the left side of my layer of three shirts, while I'm face down on the mat unable to un-crumple my body. He says, "Whoa."

I say, "What do you see?"

Phil replies, "Your rib's dislocated."

I respond, "Please put them back in."

Phil works on it as gently as possible after taking his four ounce gloves off. I'm breathing through the pain. He says, "You got to take it easy for while till this heals. Jody that rib was really out."

I ask, "You think they're broken, and/or dislocated?"

Phil replies, "Looked more dislocated. We will see."

We went light the rest of the night with pad work, after he put the ribs back in and wrapped my ribs with an ace bandage I had in my backpack.

About twelve days later, after Phil wraps up my ribs. Phil says, "Hey work with Derek on ground."

I reply, "Sure. Derek, I got a little rib issue on the left side. I'll let you know if something is bugging me."

Derek, "Okay, cool."

It's a Monday night at seven. We begin ground drills
then we go '*live*' on ground. I'm only a little tweaked.
But I rolled real well, and felt great. I knew I'd be sore,
but felt fine. Then I got cleaned up and went back to
work that night for two more hours and got out by ten
twenty. Afterwards I went home and said, 'hi' to
Norman and checked on the children sleeping in bed.

I get to check on who ate what, and reset the
children's lunch boxes for school the next day. I go
through our children's backpacks, checking our oldest
daughter's first grade homework and PTA notes. I go
through our youngest one's pre-K backpack as well.
Then before I eat, it is just after eleven. I go to get into
the shower and I look in the mirror.

Problem, my one rib is out. I didn't even feel it. I call
Phil, "Phil, sorry to bother you, but I kind of sort of have
a little issue."

Phil asked, "What?"

I replied, "Well, I don't know how but my left side a
rib is like way out. So when I see you Wednesday night,
could you put it back in?"

Phil replied, "Oh, yeah. It's going to hurt."

I reply, "That's okay I'll wear my mouth-guard
anyway. It doesn't hurt right now. If I didn't look in the
mirror just now I would've not had a clue."

Fast forward it is Wednesday night. I have feeling this is going to smart. I say, "Phil should we do it when I'm warmed up or after session?"

Phil says, "After. Then you'll be more warmed up and can rest afterwards." I agree.

So we have a light session of drilling. Then Phil asks, "Okay, you ready?"

I keep my mouth-guard in and lay on my stomach. I say, "I'll try not to yell. Warn your wife."

Phil sees it and applies whatever pressure to put it back in. I freak him out with a yelp. "I'm sorry Phil. Here try again. I'll stay still." I bite down on my mouth-guard. "FUUUUUUCK! Oh God. Did you get it back in?"

Phil replies, "Yeah, that was nasty."

I respond, "You're telling me. I think I saw God."

From then on we taped me before every practice for about the next three plus years.

Socially Awkward

His social ineptness,
Kept him hid.

Yet he was not,
The only kid.

No one knew,
What was his plight.

That kept such a boy,
As a man from flight.

For they herded others,
And not his voice.

To come from so many,
Was not his choice.

As no attention,
Was paid to him.

That's how it was,
In the days of dim.

No diagnosis,
Would they give.

No mercy be shown,
To disease he'd have.

Figure 3. Ground Game

Chapter Nineteen
The Smack Heard Round the World

It was cold January night, a Monday after seven o'clock. Phil's basement gym was packed. Rashid whom some of the guys knew from a local high school years before was to spar that night. In walked Rashid into Phil's Basement Gym about a month or so back. Phil made certain that this incredible specimen of an athlete would be given a chance.

Rashid, a heavy-weight for certain, had some boxing experience. Yet, it didn't appear to me that he had much ground game at the time. It almost seemed like he hit so hard that he didn't need a ground game.

He was fast, agile, and reeked of athletic prowess. I thought to myself, 'Maybe this guy is going to be Phil's breakthrough fighter.' Funny thing is that Phil never ever spoke that way about fighters, with reference to himself. He was there solely for the fighters and people interested in helping themselves.

I knew I had to train that night. However, I wanted to watch Rashid, and Gregg spar. But, I was sent to the back corner into the boxing ring to work ground with another guy, who weighed 170 pounds. He was close to my age, and he had a good wrestling background. Phil really wanted me to work more ground that night. So I complied. The people he originally wanted to put me with, one came late and one was really, 'not all there'.

I'd heard that Gregg was an animal. I couldn't wait to meet Gregg. I'd not ever seen Gregg spar, but heard the stories. Rashid I'd seen spar very lightly, tonight was the night. Phil was testing Rashid.

Gregg and Rashid were about the same size in weight and in height. So Phil could not be disturbed. He had to watch these men carefully, coaching them as they went. They were both heavy-hitters and didn't seem to care about damage, when that's present, it's a beautiful thing to watch.

The front section of the cage was roped off for Gregg and Rashid. The next section was roped off for a few guys doing round robin *stand up*. And the section after that next to the boxing ring, which then created a kind of 'L' shape to the room for fighting had about six guys in it doing ground.

The gym was really active. Before Gregg and Rashid began to spar about thirty minutes of the classes' session had already passed. Then Gregg and Rashid began to go at it.

The 170 pound wrestler type and I had been training already for those thirty minutes. We were so focused, that we are not distracted by the sparring match of Gregg and Rashid's, for the most part.

In the beginning, we all were busy doing what we came in for. Then as natural, as a fight breaks out…Gregg and Rashid begin to spar everyone stops what they're doing and watches.

Everyone else is doing drills right now, and so everyone is minding their business and training. The two of us are in the ten foot by ten foot ring. I'm submitting this guy a lot. And I have been working ground with him for the better part of the last three months.

Unknowingly to me at the time, he supposedly had said, and done annoying things to the other guys in the gym. that he had worked with in the past. I'm so used to that with some guys who walk through Phil's basement gym cage doors, that I'm barely phased by it. Others complain, that they won't work with this guy. But I'm cool with it. I actually feel kind of sorry for him. You see over the past three months that I've worked with him, I found out he's got kids, and he is divorced. And it's rather an unpleasant set of circumstances for him.

Phil always wonders how I get this kind of information out of people. My husband says, "You always manage to get guys talking and telling you everything." Yeah, I do. I guess I care too much. I hate to see loneliness. Why? Perhaps, I do understand loneliness. I also understand someone who has struggled in their lives from social awkwardness, and comprehension issues as well. They are usually smarter than most.

The first sixty minutes we are grappling (ground fighting), I submit him ten times. He submits me once. The class is ninety minutes long. He's frustrated. I can tell by him getting rougher with his *takedowns* and slams on me.

Then even worse, he thinks he has a submission. I tell him he doesn't. And there as he stands, and holds my left leg in the air, where he thinks he has a heel hook. I am on my back on the ground, and I'm not tapping. It's not a heel hook, I'm trying to tell him as he twisting my foot, and cranks the lower leg. In doing so, then I feel a searing pain. I don't tap. I've snapped my left peroneus longus. Upon him getting frustrated, I then get out of his hold. I know I'm damaged but I stand up, and he has no clue. He's pissed.

Then he says, "Hey let's go look. The guys are watching Gregg and Rashid. They've stopped using that space over there. We will have more room. Let's wrestle there."

I respond, "Okay. You want to work there?"

He responds, "Yeah. That's a great space."

We move over to outside the ten by ten foot ring, where we have a lot more room. And no one seems to mind.

It now seems like he realizes that doing rough *takedowns* on me doesn't seem to phase me. So he starts tapping my head to distract me before the *takedown* attempt. Only it's not a tap, it becomes more like a slap. The slaps increase so much that they become hard smacks upside my head. He does this I think, because now he can't get an angle on me.

So his tapping to my head, which then become hard smacks to my head, become harder and harder. By the seventh smack, I get pissed.

Finally, stopping him, I say real loud, "Hey, you're smacking me, that's no tap! You want a smack. I'll give you a smack. *Com'on!*"

I lunge at him, and opening my right hand, whole hand connects smacking him as hard as I can upside the left side of his head. As I do that, I yell totally enraged, "FUUUUUUCK YOOUUUUUUU!"

And yes, I am ready to beat this guy silly. By this time, I guess he realizes I'm not afraid of him. As he is running away from what may appear to be rabid wolf, or a wolverine, "I don't want none of that!" He states, with fear in his voice.

Before I know it, Phil is right in front of me, "What happened?"

I stop immediately, I can't believe I was so angry, "Sorry Phil. But I let him slam me a bunch. Then I let him slap me, then he started smacking me upside the head. Then the smacks got harder. Seven times Phil, to the right side of the head. It wasn't right. So I figured if he wanted to smack instead of wrestle with me. I'd dish it back to him. Sorry Phil." I hung my head, "I kind of lost it."

Phil said, "Okay."
Upon the profanity and sound of the smack I landed, the whole gym stopped. All activity was halted temporarily. People were in shock or so it seemed. Little did I know what was going through everyone's mind.
Things seemed to get back to normal. The smacked guy left. I stayed. This all happened near the end of session.

Then one of big cops who'd fought came over to me. He said, "I was about to take him and just throw his body outside of the gym. I can't stand the guy."

I responded, "Really?" I did not know really why many of the other guys had not worked with him in the past three months.

He replied, "Oh yeah. He's a jerk." I breathed a slight sigh of relief. Soon enough the class session was over and there was only three of us.

Phil said, "Jody, what we do here. What happened is normal. Your response was normal. And it's my fault."

I responded, "Huh? But I lost my temper. I don't like that, and I'm usually not like that. It takes a lot for me to lose it like that, Phil."

Phil continued, "I put you with him for the last three months because he aggravated everyone. You were the last holdout. Peter had a tough time with him. He insulted guys, and pulled the same stuff on them. The guys all complained about him. You. You never complain. For you to lose your temper. I know he was taunting you. It's my fault. It's not you."

I responded, "So I'm okay here?"

Phil replied, "Yes, don't worry about it. If he comes back I will explain to him, that he must behave."

I say, "You know he's got kids. He's divorced. I actually feel sorry for him."

Phil replied, "Yes, he is a bit socially awkward. But he is old enough to know better. It's not you. He needs to behave."

I respond, "Talk to him. I think he needs this gym Phil."

Phil replied, "I will."

The next night, Tuesday, January 5th, the guy comes in when I'm not there. Phil sits him down, and speaks with him. The next night I have a private session with Phil, "How did it go?"

Phil replies, "I explained to him he was ready to get kicked out of the gym after that by a bunch of the guys. And I was going to kick him out too. I told him that you did not dislike him. But that he had to behave. He said, 'okay'. He did seem surprised that I did not kick him out of the gym."

I responded, "That's good he needs this place. Right now I think he needs to train with others. So I can cool off."

Phil replied, "Yeah, I'm sorry. I won't do that to you again."

I respond, "No problem."

Later that year, this man really became a great teammate. Phil and I realized this guy's social awkwardness was not due to him being of bad character. But rather we felt, and knew we were correct, that he had a undiagnosed set of circumstances that were ignored. So he was ignored. He'd come from a big family as well. The man was our age.

Eventually, as time passed his life began to improve. He regained a relationship with his children, primarily his son. The man got his I.Q. tested. Which I hoped would happen for him.

A few years later, one night, after he'd had gone through a positive life-altering experience. We were in the cage working ground together, now at Phil's new big Gym, '*Asylum Fight Gym*'.

We were working me passing his guard. We were drilling it, over and over again. Finally he says, "I got my I.Q. checked."

I respond, "Really? What was it?"

He replied, "*Ahhhh.* I'm kind of smart. My son is too." He expresses a bashful, 'awe shucks' look on his face and body language shows his reluctance.

I ask, "*Com'on.* Tell me. I bet it is real high."

He responds, "Yeah, I guess. It was 157. My son's is higher." He smiles, as he shakes his head.

I smile and say, "I knew you were really smart."

He asks, "How did you know that?"

I respond, "Because of the way you acted. And I could relate to how you feel socially. You know what I mean?"

He said, "Really?"

I reply, "Yeah, I really get it. It's tough sometimes. You know. And *hec*. I'm only 130. So you're doing great. Man, that's just awesome! Good for you. I got to say I'm proud of you."

After this time, it's not all his problems would go away. Yet, it was that his life had become a little sweeter. And Phil and I knew, that not everyone could appreciate his way. But those intelligent enough, and forgiving teammates accepted his oddities. I can say as much as I miss the old group we had all those basement gym years, I think I miss him the most.

Figure 4. Phil wrapping Rashid in New York

Jody-Lynn Reicher

The Age Noone Heard

She began to dream,
As it did seem.
At an age more then some.

Her pursuit of a goal,
Embedded dormant in her soul.
Arose one day with the sun.

She stood in shape,
Before men not in cape.
Her willingness would though stun.

Some men would girl-up,
Because she wouldn't curl up.
Her fists flying with such fun.

Her eyes they would blacken,
And in turn she would crack them.
Their volley of punches did flow.

The lessons she learned,
A fighter they turned.
Her brawler to some technical so.

Men came and went,
Many did vent.
She's too small, too old, and too slow.

She continued on,
Other's bewilderment did spawn.

About her lacks too many to know.

Some people would gripe,
How did she get those fights?
All the while, their willingness lay low.

"It's how hard you train".
She tried to explain.
"Maintaining your goals in full scope".

Chapter Twenty
NAGA World Championships April 10th 2010

In April 2010 in Newark, New Jersey there was a NAGA World Championship Grappling event. Again, Phil and I decided to enter me in as many divisions as possible.

We were preparing me for my entry into Mixed Martial Arts competitions. Grappling, would be one of the three areas of discipline for fighting in an MMA event. So we entered me into four women's divisions and two men's divisions. We were trying to get as many opponents for me as close to my weight-class as possible. I weighed in the morning of competition at 106 pounds.

The two men's divisions for beginners were: Open (open meaning ages eighteen and up, usually to age thirty) category, weight-class of 120 to 129.9 pounds, and Open category at weight-class of 130 to 139.9 pounds. The women's were the over forty division at weight-class of 140 to 140.9 pounds, was Expert (Expert is over five years experience) Division. The women's open divisions; where no one was under 125 pounds, and the women's division ages thirty to thirty-nine at weight class 140 to 149.9 pounds. Then there were Absolute (all classes, weights, and ages) Women's matches as well.

Since I was a Beginner, which is measured by time learning, and competing combined in doing grappling competitions (ground fighting), which is zero to eighteen months experience.

I had to forgo the men's Beginner Open division 120 to129.9 pound matches because one of the women's matches of 140 to 149.9 pounds was going on at the same time. I won the Gold in the Intermediate (Intermediate meaning usually two to five years experience) Division for ages thirty- to thirty-nine at the weight-class of 140 to 149.9 pounds.

I then won the Silver in the Women's Expert ages forty to forty-nine, at the weight class division 140-149.9 pounds. I won the Bronze in the Men's Beginner Open (ages eighteen and up) Division, at the weight-class of 130 to 139.9 pounds. I was still a Beginner, it was not yet eighteen months that I'd been training and competing in Grappling.

The next time I went to compete in June 2010, I was banned from entering the Men's Divisions of anything. I wondered why. Well, not really. When I went to see my results from NAGA tournaments, they had my name and they did not record what gender I was in the men's division.

Winning the Bronze put a few men in a quiet uproar. My argument to them would be, *'It is unlikely that a 105 pound woman is going to attack me and rape me. This was good self-defense practice. Never mind dealing with different body types'*. And the fact I really only had men to train with all this time. And I had only been submitted once in sixteen men's matches.

The matches at NAGA World Championship where I'd earned the Bronze Medal in the Men's Division, Beginner, Open, weight-class of 130 to 139.9 pounds was the first time in fifty-two matches I was beaten by a submission.

The opponent was a young man, age thirty-two, 137 pounds and five feet and nine inches tall. He was tattooed, shaved, no shirt, and slick as heck. Nicest guy in the world. Very sweet. We actually enjoyed the two minutes plus we grappled together. Right from the beginning of the match I knew this was going to be a fun person to compete against. We smiled at each other, slapped hands and went at it. We clinched three times, and three times I broke the clinch. He did a classic BJJ (Brazilian Ju Jitsu) move. After two minutes plus he brought me down to the ground, and submitted me with an arm-bar.

I said to this nice young man, nearly sixteen years my junior, "You're the first person to submit me in over fifty matches." He smiled, hugged me, and I wished him 'Good Luck' in his Gold Medal round. He's the only man in competition to date this book being published, to have ever submitted me in a Grappling match.

Since then I accumulated ninety-five matches in all. I won a Silver Medal at the Grapplers Quest World Championship 119.9 pounds and under, Women's Open Expert Division December 13, 2013.

Figure 5. Peter and Phil at Asylum Fight Gym

Jody-Lynn Reicher

Diversity Is Safer

It's not that we,
Desire much.
For so many,
Can be out of touch.

It is what makes,
Our vines so strong,
For our nation,
Diversity does belong.

It is a necessity,
Others so deny.
Feeling superiority,
Rights taken will decry.

Old guard panics,
As not one had spied.
They're above it,
Claiming others lied.

One day when,
We become mature.
America will become safer,
In diversity for sure.

Chapter Twenty-One
Who Are We…? (2010)

After Peter Dell'Orto takes his mouth-guard out, he put it best. Looking at Phil he says, "…A third of us wear the badge. A third of us have a rap-sheet, and a third of us are just well… However, we seem to all get along." Peter, a tall Caucasian man, stood six feet four inches, weighing between 183 to 190 pounds. Very light-skinned as a Polish and Northern Italian man can be.

Here is a man just recently married to a very petite well-educated Japanese woman. They are both well-educated. He is an ESL (English as a Second Language) Teacher, a translator. Peter is conversationally capable in Japanese. He's written multiple PDF files for software and software for games and the like. He is a certified trainer. He's fought in Japan. That is stand up. He lived in Japan for a good amount of years as well.

Peter is probably, one of the most considerate people who you'd ever meet. If he says he's going to be somewhere at some time, he'll be there. If he's sick he'll say so, so he doesn't breed his germs. When he's sick, he takes care and gets better quicker than anyone I've ever seen with few exceptions.

And how he described Phil's basement gym? Well Peter was correct. Everyone that walked into Phil's basement gym were all of different backgrounds, Hasidic, Muslim, Catholic, Atheist, it didn't matter. Every skin tone, and every continent was represented. And there, you could go to war if you wanted to.

I can say you learn a lot about people, when there is such diversity. And then you begin to learn a lot about yourself. That's the beauty of diversity. In the gym, we all sweat and bleed equally, when we put our minds to it.

At the end of sessions, some guys would relax a bit and hang out. They'd be making conversation on all different levels. Sometimes it occurred before session while guys were warming up and stretching.

Many of the conversations were not ones that I had ever really heard completely, until then. However, it opened doors for me. Phil would say to me, "You know, it's funny. When you are here, we don't even know a woman has entered or is training here."

I responded, "Really?"

Phil continued one day, "Yeah. You arrive, enter and there's no change in the room. No female giggle. Nothing that says, *'a female has entered this gym'*."

I respond, "Wow. I guess that's good. I try to do that. I did that in the Marines, I know I did."

One day Leif and I were grappling and he said, "I love ground. If it's going to be a fight. In a street, I want it on the ground."

I responded, "Wow. Not me, man. I want it stand-up, and then beat him on the ground. Why?"

Then Leif began to tell me a childhood story. A story that told me a lot about his childhood and upbringing.

He began wrestling at around age fourteen. Leif had good ground and was very creative. His thought process was genius. He was shy, quiet, proper, and caring. He was a *Golden Gloves Champion*. But he would never volunteer that information to you. He and his wife rescued pit bulls. He disliked greatly cruelty to anything living.

One day I found out when his fortieth birthday was. I went out and bought him and his wife four cupcakes, in four different colors. They were *Cookie Monster* cupcakes, made by a local bakery. I said, "I didn't know what colors you and your wife like. So I bought all four colors they had. Hope you like them."

The thing that told me that Leif had a high I.Q. was that one day he brought in a book, written by a physiologist. Leif said, "I've read this book. I would like to lend it to you for a week. Read pages sixteen to forty-three."

I responded, "Wow! Thank you. I will." I took the book. I read those pages about four times that week. It was brilliant. He was onto something. This same book, I've turned so many people onto to this day. I cannot remember how many people I referred this book to. This book is a part of my life to this very day. And when you step into my treatment room, it's included in how I question the client/pain patient and how I see human anatomy. Just those pages has changed so many lives in my office, it is beyond belief.

As time passed, Leif got a new job and had much travelling at time to do. He and his wife had no children, but they took care of the dogs they adopted very well, I can say.

Unknown at first to me, his final breath was on Saturday September 17th, 2011 on a highway late that night. Leif apparently exhausted from work and having to drive about three or more hours that night to get home, fell asleep at the wheel. It was a single car crash and a single fatality, his.

To this day, I know how much I miss Leif. I know Tom, Steve, and Peter miss him much as well. The four of us when we've trained together even to this day as I write this just before publishing this book, at the end of March 2017. One of us says to one another, "What was that thing Leif would do? He always had an idea." And we would start to dissect a move Leif was good at.

Figure 6. Kyle Rigby wins the Title February 2010

Sets Her Free

It's irrelevant so you see,
Ageless benevolence sets her free.

Many want to pigeon-hole,
To stop the living of one's own soul.

The outsiders see it not as sin,
Yet as a way to keep down kin.

For if they let such ones arise,
Their laziness will show to their surprise.

Figure 7. Atlantic City, NJ First Fight

Chapter Twenty-Two
October 8th 2010

"Phil, when am I going to get a fight? I'm really desperate." I asked.

"I'm trying." Phil responded.

"I'm just afraid that time will pass and I'll never get a fight. I need one bad." I reiterated.

"Okay. Don't worry. I'm working on it." Phil answered.

Then about three weeks later, Phil says, "Looks like you got a girl that wants to fight you down in Atlantic City at Scott Morgan's show *New Breed Fighters* in October."

"Oh thank God." I reply.

"Now, you'll need medicals. Since you are over forty you have to get extra medicals, besides a physical, an eye exam, a gynecological exam, you'll need an MRI and an MRA, a Stress-Test, and a Carotid Doppler Test. Oh, also a blood test for pregnancy, HIV, Hep C and Hep B." Phil added.

"Okay, I have to see how I'm going to get the money together. I'll call my internist on the basics." I remarked.

Phil continues, "Also you have to write a letter to the Athletic Commissioner of the State of New Jersey, explaining why you want to fight."

I respond, "Really?"

Phil responds, 'Yep. I'll tell you what he wants. I know him. He seems really reluctant to allow this fight. It's because of your age. Also he hasn't had an amateur MMA female fight yet in Atlantic City I believe."

I ask, "So this would be the first?"

Phil responded, "Well, there has been professional MMA female fights in Atlantic City."

So I get busy figuring out funding, then I realize I have a $2,000 bond I won in 1986 from a five mile race. I held onto this particular item for an emergency just like this. This way I wouldn't be taking out from my family, or from my business. It was like found money, which I had forgotten about. I called Phil back.

Phil says, "The Deputy Athletic Commissioner said to go to his doctors down near Vineland, New Jersey. Jody they'll give you a good deal on all of it."

I respond, "Including a full physical?"

Phil replies, "Yes." Then Phil receives all the places I have to go to and I set up all the appointments. I have to take two days off of work, training etc…to get all this done. I end up going to five or six places way down south, about two hours from my home for all the exams. In the end it costs me about $2,000. I was in better than perfect condition. However, they could barely get a reading on the stress test at the hospital down south there.

Thank God the Cardiac Doctor who was doing the test, was a long distance runner. My running mileage at the time was down to 110 miles a week, and that week was 85 miles of running. As soon as they got me off the treadmill, my pulse would zip down to forty-three, that was by the time they'd lay me on the table for a reading within thirty seconds.

I've had a very low pulse especially early in the morning. I was there by six o'clock that morning. I'd drove, yet, hadn't really woken up completely yet. Even after two hours of driving, and an empty stomach for urine and blood tests later in the day. My real cup of coffee was running ten miles or so before I start my day usually.

After everything was poked, prodded, tested, medical staff were shaking their heads. "Not on any medication, you're really fit for someone almost forty-eight years old." I thought to myself, '*well that's nice. Tell the State of New Jersey that. Would you please?*'

It was an exhausting process. I had two days of driving down and back for all the medical tests and going from place for an appointment to the next, in an area of the state I was a little unfamiliar with.

Thank God it was two weeks or so before the event was to take place. Now Phil and I had to wait for the results. Every part of me had to be perfect. Amazingly, I went through the process without a bruise before-hand. We continued training me, and within about a week, we had all of the results. *It was a go.* I'm cleared to fight and the Deputy Athletic Commissioner liked my letter. He accepts my reasons for training and fighting in a cage. My opponent Rachel Sazoff is cleared as well. She is age twenty, and this is her first fight as well.

Her background I'm told is that she started Tae Kwon Do around age six. She's a third degree black belt. She started wrestling about seven or eight years before and competed on her high school boys wrestling team all four years. She started boxing training a while ago.

My experience to the contrary is the fight was sixteen days before I turn age forty-eight. I had been running and competing since age thirteen. I walked around weight between 103 and 106 pounds. Sazoff walks around much more in the 120 pound range. The fight is set at 112 to 118 pounds. How I got there...A lot of water right before weigh-ins.

The background I had in any form of wrestling were three afternoons of lessons in December of 1978 from Joanne Yelloweyes, a friend of mine. Joanne was a Shoshone Indian from Montana. My martial art experience was a handful of sessions in August 1985 in Okinawan Karate, Rick Rohrman's Budokai Karate dojo. I didn't like bowing and kneeling, so I quit.

And then February 2009, started to learn ground. Then we started training me for ground competition in late March 2009. Phil's ground style was *Gamu*. Then I started Phil's Burmese Boxing, *Hykien/Kachin* style fighting stand-up in July 2009. So by the time the fight day would arrive, which was Friday, October 8th, 2010, I had just over eighteen months ground experience. Which this included just over fifteen months of stand-up training, along with other martial art forms cumulatively throughout my nearly forty-eight years.

She, Sazoff had over fourteen years in total in Martial Arts, about eight or more years in ground training. She had a Brown Belt in BJJ (Brazilian Ju Jitsu), soon to receive her Black Belt. And I was told she had Boxing training as well, to boot.

On Tuesday night October 5th, 2010, Scott Morgan, Rachel Sazoff, Phil, and I were invited by Miguel Castro to go on the air on his '*Liquid Lightening*' Internet Radio Talk Show. Sazoff last minute could not make it in person, so she called in, as we were on the air for Castro to bring her on the '*air*'.

We were on the air for seemingly about ninety minutes. People called in, and questions were answered. People wanted to know my fighting experience. I answered, "Well, I had an older brother who was the prince. So if you picked on him, and I was around, I'd beat you up." I almost snort laughed when I said this. But that was my mentality.

Sazoff recanted her saying she was going to knock me out in the first round. As if it was going to be an easy fight. She kept her talk neutral. Which I thought was smart of her.

Later, privately Phil told me what she was predicting and saying the week before the radio show.

"What did she say?" I asked Phil.

"She said, she 'would knock you out in the first minute or so of the first round'." Phil replied.

I asked, 'What do you think?"

Phil responded, "Well, word has it, she thinks she can. I really don't think so. We heard how she's training stand-up. She's wearing headgear and big gloves, like boxing. That's how she trains stand-up with marshmallows protecting her." Meanwhile Phil had me training like the men in his gym. They almost always had trained with four ounce gloves, shin guards, mouth guard and no head gear.

I reply, "Well, I think you need the reality of getting whacked, to keep your hands up to your face, with the four ounce gloves on. Because I think it gets you use to getting hit. Right?"

Phil responds, "Yeah. That's what I think. It's less shocking if you're use to it. And the adrenalin rush does a number on some people. Now you're changing how it feels to get hit on top of that. Also she's sparring with smaller guys than you are."

I reply, "Oh yeah. None of our guys are under 158 pounds usually. I'm working primarily with 160 to 190 pound guys on stand-up and ground."

As the day approached I felt confident I'd be heavy enough. I was gaining weight like never before. Then Thursday arrived, I weighed 109.5 pounds. I had to make 112.1 pounds and be within three pounds of Sazoff's weight. I was a little nervous, but I figured I'd be okay. The weigh-ins would be about four hours before our fight.

Phil was still up in Northern Jersey on Thursday, October 7th. I was in a hotel room in Atlantic City. The next day, fight morning, Friday morning I went out for a little five mile run. I had done this all my ground fighting competitions. I'd run between four and ten miles in the morning before every tournament. It helped me sort things out mentally.

I got back to my hotel room and ate a big breakfast, I was starving. Then I weighed myself. "*Ahhhhh.* What 108.8 pounds. You're kidding me." I said out loud to myself. I called Phil.

Panicked I said, "Phil, I'm getting skinny again. What do I do?"

Phil responded, "Don't' worry. You'll be fine. I'll be down there this afternoon. I *gotta* wrap a few lose ends up."

I responded, "Okay." I began to drink more water.

I laid back down on the bed and drank some water, closed my eyes and passed out. I was hyper, then exhausted. Tired, yet up. The emotions ebbed and flowed. They were positive, yet my insides see-sawed. A couple hours later, I weighed myself again. I had brought our own scale that we were use to weighing me on. I lost weight again. I was 108.5 pounds.

By the time Phil got there I was 107.6 pounds. My insides were dying. I thought, 'this could kill the fight.' I didn't know how much water was too much. I had no clue.

Soon enough Phil had arrived, to our hotel. Then we drove over to the place where the fights would take place, it was *Resorts Casino*, Atlantic City. I was losing weight. That was due to nerves. We weighed me early, so we could gage how much weight I needed to gain. We were trying to figure out how much Sazoff weighed as she walked around. We guessed she was 115 pounds. Then we had to get me to 112.1 pounds. So it would be add water to *the Jody*, weigh *the Jody*. Add water to *the Jody*, weigh *the Jody*. Then after getting the Jody to spec, relax. Don't move.

Then came the weigh-ins. I can't remember what I weighed exactly, I know it was over 112.1 pounds. Sazoff weighed within two pounds of me. Next was the *rules meeting*. Then the doctor does a once over. He checks the pulse, blood pressure and such. The doctor that was present saw my age on the fight paper. The doctor was a white haired medical doctor of about age sixty-eight to seventy-two years. He began to ask questions.

Then he says, "Your pulse is fifty-two." Looking shocked.

Phil responds, "She runs 100 miles a week."

The doctor then says, "Your blood pressure is one twenty over seventy-two."

I respond, "Well that's high for me. I'm like ninety-eight over sixty-eight."

The doctor in finishing asks, "Why are you doing this. Is it a bucket list?"

Phil jumps in and says, "No. She's not like that. She is a fighter."

The doctor smiles, as he raised a brow. He doesn't seem to know what to say. Then he asks me, "Is that correct?"

I respond, "Yes. That would be correct."

Time ebbs and flows. We have other guys on the fight card. After Phil wraps my hands, they are signed by the officials. We are in this dimly lit conference room type section of the hotel. The carpeting is a swirly design, the drapery is red. They have these areas sectioned off in this big conference room, so you can train and drill without people seeing you right before your fight.

We are in the middle of all the fights. There are about fifteen fights or so. We do some warm up drills. I will be called out first, then Sazoff will get her opening call. I'm walking out to *Creedence Clearwater Revival's* song, *"Fortunate Son"*. I thought it was appropriate, yet very tongue in cheek. Phil and Peter liked it.

We are taken through this backstage area before the fights begin. It is to introduce each fighter on the fight card in fight card order. They do filming and take pictures of the fighters for the promotion during this time.

As I wait in the conference room staging area, after that walk through for the fight promotion. I'm resting in the conference room set up for us with the carpeting and the drapes. In walk two friends, not fighters. Dr. Dan Schaefer and Barrie Sue. They tell me that they have a good feeling about this fight. That I will do well. I thank them. They wish me luck and head out to the audience.

Then as the fights begin, my fight is number eight. We have to await other fights to be completed in order for me to get the official shin guards and four ounce gloves on, that are provided. Everything is regulated.

By the time they call for the fourth fight, the next set of gloves I get are men's mediums. They are too small. The people working the table where the shin guards and gloves are sanitized, recorded, taken in, and given out, cannot believe I need a men's large set of gloves. Phil can't believe it. But they just fit right.

The shin guards just came off a body they sprayed them with Lysol and then I'm handed a pair of wet shin guards. They're wet with sweat and Lysol. I think, 'Oh well. Beggars can't be choosy.'

Then Phil has me warm up with big Kyle. Phil does some warm-up with me as well. Then we rest a little; then a little more warm-up, again. It takes a lot for me to warm-up. I'm cooling down so fast, which is usual for me under any athletic competitive circumstances.

And I now know after three hours and six trips to the bathroom, I'm probably weighing 106 pounds. I like skinny. Feeling light for an event does make me feel better. I feel ready. The promotion lets us know I'm on deck. One more fight and I will take the walk, to see what kind of fighter I am and what's in the tank.

Soon that moment comes. They play *Creedence Clearwater Revival's "Fortunate Son"*, and I start to take the walk. The inertia of the cage pulled me into it. To the point, as I took the walk down I almost ran down during the walk out. I was nearly ahead of my crew. I figured, '*what the hec. I'm doing this*'. The butterflies that were in my stomach, and in my body were no longer. There was no fear. I told myself, '*stay in your own music, even during her walkout*'.

Before I knew it, Phil, the guys, and I are at the cage. They are checking my mouth-guard, body pat down, etc… After hugs, Phil applies grease to my face, I step up into the cage. I am told where to stand. Now I'm alone for what seems seconds.

Then Sazoff gets announced. I can say I don't remember anything, but the fight. I even cannot recall the instructions Don the referee told me. He instructed us to start, and I just went. I got sixty-five percent across the cage floor and then we strike. I was determined to throw as much as possible.

I knew her ground game was good; especially compared to mine. But I felt I could easily take a punch, and I don't mind getting hit. And this is why Phil had trained me as hard as he did. Because I was willing and he was able. Phil was is able to handle training someone who fights raw, whether male or female. And that's what he called me months before. Phil said, "You are just raw."

I then asked, "What do you mean?"

Phil replied, "If you can't punch someone in the face. You punch back. When you see a neck, you automatically go for the guillotine."

I asked, "Really?"

Phil repeated, "Yes. You are just raw."

I replied, "So I'm like Mungo. Me throw body."

Phil replied, "Yes. And that's raw."

The first round ends, she got mount, but no damage. Phil says, "She got that round."

I reply, "Okay. Yeah I thought so." I pop up from the stool. I don't like to rest. I like to keep going like I do in the gym, where I will go at times for up to forty-five minutes sparring with Phil. Or the guys will do five to fifteen minutes with me in a row. *Time is on my side*, I think.

Then Phil points out, "She's already breathing heavy."

I reply, "Oh yeah."

Phil says, "Okay, be aggressive."

I reply, "Yep."

I come out faster than I did in the first round. I may have gone further to her side but I'm not certain. I'm now warmed up. We fight. She attempts to stand up with me. Her corner, does not want her to stand-up with me.

I somehow get her up against the cage. I'm throwing punches, but I haven't mastered much else other than jab and cross. The referee warns her that he's going to call it a TKO, "Rachel, you *gotta* do something…!" He reminds her.

Later I found out if I had known how to throw a hook in my combinations, I would've had her, and gotten a TKO in the second round. But that was not to be. I just was too inexperienced. Then she somehow as I paused, trying to figure out what else to throw. During my happy brain-fart she then dove in, and got a take down.

I knew that she got points for that. So, I just focused on moving out of that position. Before I knew it, round two ended and I was back in the corner. I heard Phil's voice, "Jody she got that *takedown*. This round was better for you. You almost had her."

I reply, "Yeah."

Phil reminds me, "Be aggressive."

I ask, "How'm I doin'?"

Phil responds, 'Good. But you got to not let her get the *takedown*."

I respond, "Okay."

I'm up off the stool before time is up. She's still seated. I hear a noise, it lets me know they want us to get ready for the third and final round. And then before I know it we're at it again, fighting.

It is just as physical as the other two rounds were. However, this time as I jump on her with punching, she pushes me towards the other side of the cage. Time passes as we fight. She gets me down again. With about twelve seconds to go I reverse her and begin to throw knees on ground to her legs and hips. The bell sounds it's the end of the fight.

I walk over my corner and Phil says, "You lost to a decision."

I reply, "Yeah, I know. I'm sorry."

Then we are gathered to the center of the cage and Don the referee stands there holding our hands, awaiting the decision from the judges.

And Don says, "You look like you're ready for more."

I respond, "Can I do another one tonight? That was really fun." We laugh. Sazoff does not appear so happy. I couldn't read her.

I remembered, I was told that she told people she was going to knock me out in the first round. And I'm nearly forty-eight, and she is twenty years old. I don't look at things like that, till someone points it out to me. I saw it

177

as, we fought she did more better things than I did, and won.

After it is over, we all shake hands and such. And I am the first one to exit off the stage. There are guys in suits to my left clapping and a couple police officers, I shake their hands and as I come off the stage I see two young men. They are looking at me in earnest.

These two are at the very end of the stairs and at the beginning of the front row aisle. The one to the left is about six feet one inch tall and weighs about four hundred pounds. He seems to be about age twenty-four. He wears glasses, a baseball cap, jeans, short sleeved shirt and appears shy.

The young man about the same age to his left, appears to be same height, same glasses, same jeans, same shirt, same baseball cap, yet is about one hundred sixty-five pounds. He is holding a camera in his hand and he is smiling, looking straight at me.

As I approach, the skinny young man calls out, "Hey, my friend here is afraid to ask you. He would like to take a picture with you."

I am so flattered, I smile, shake the young man's hand, and say "Sure thing". I wrap my arm around the bigger of the two young men and say, "Come here honey." I hug him. The skinny young man takes pictures and then I give the big young man a peck on the cheek. Phil seeing this from afar. Phil is behind me. I'm just going through the crowd, people are touching me. People are shaking their heads as they shake my hand, and smiling. I thought to myself, '*Wow, they really enjoyed it. I guess I did okay. How neat.*'

After we get through the crowds and across the hallway to get my gear off and for them to announce the next fight, I stand in line to return the gloves and shin guards. I asked, "Hey Phil, too cute. You see those two boys when I got down from the stairs? Man, they were just so cute. The two of them. They wanted pictures with me. That was so cute. That was so nice."

Phil replies, "Jody, I got to tell you something. Fighters especially when they lose they don't smile that much. Or do that."

I respond, "Well, they seemed nice, they asked. And it made them happy. Why wouldn't I be happy?"

Phil responded, "Well, fighters win or lose aren't usually like that."

I asked, "But why? I mean like, if it weren't for them we wouldn't have an audience to perform in front of. Right?"

Phil responded, "Yeah, it's good what you did. But most fighters think only of themselves after a fight."

I ask, "Hey, Phil can I go watch the rest of the fights?"

Phil responded, "Yes. That's a good idea."

After we get the gear squared away and I bring an extra top with me we return to the area where the audience is. As I walk in, people still recognize me, they stop me, smile, and shake my hand. They can't believe my age. I'm shocked at their remembering me.

Phil goes to talk to someone. Finally, I can take a seat. Then a referee comes up to me and he leans in smiling at me, puts his hand out to shake my hand and says, "That was just amazing. You're so inspirational. You give me hope."

I respond, "Well, Thank you."

Then a woman from another fight team who is a spectator says, "That was amazing. I now think maybe I can do that. I've been doing grappling for a while and thought I could never get in a cage and fight."

I ask, "Well how old are you?"

She responds, "Thirty-seven, and I thought I was too old. I guess I'm not. You're forty-seven, right?"

I reply, "Well actually in sixteen days I'll be forty-eight."

She responded, "I heard you had about only eighteen months of training."

I replied, "Yes, that's about right."

She responded, "Well, I have to go and get back to my teammates now. But thanks for talking to me."

I reply, "My pleasure." We shake hands and she departs. I stay seated there, wondering if my opponent will come out into the audience as I had.

Just then I see Phil, we chat and I ask him, "Hey did Rachel come out to the audience yet?"

Phil responds, "You know, I don't think so. But it is a good thing to do."

I was pretty high that whole night on the experience, so much so, that when I got back to hotel I had to go for a run after I took a shower. I spoke with my husband before he went to bed. Norman said, "That was great. You two kept it going. It was not boring."

I reply, "Oh, that's good to hear…"

Then I said 'good-bye' to Norman. And soon enough I was out running it was about one thirty in the morning. It was nice out. I got in just under eight miles, running by the bay that surrounded one portion of the hotel we stayed by.

Days later, back in the gym, the guys congratulated me. They saw the fight on line and thought I did good. Then a week passed and Keith was working with Big Pat. Just before the Saturday group session, Keith said, "Jody, you did good. I have to tell you, I really am impressed that you did so well against a black belt and someone with so much more experience. I didn't expect it."

Figure 8. First Fight picture our youngest daughter drew.

Chapter Twenty-Three
She's Psychedelic (December 1st, 2010)

I was having continuing problems throwing the cross (usually the dominant handed punch), the way Phil wanted me to. At home I'd practiced practically every night, and doing so I developed a habit of looking down. This was to see if my feet were in the correct structure and if my rear foot turned as I threw that punch.

So one Monday night class, it was December 1st, 2010 at seven o'clock. Phil is doing pads with me. Then Phil says, "You want to *move*?"

I respond, "Uh, Yeah sure."

Phil goes to the bin, as I pray under my breath. Phil gets a pair of matching four ounce MMA gloves and puts them on and we begin to spar. I wanted to show him, that I had been training on my new water bag at home that weighs about 270 pounds. I bought it for just over one hundred dollars as a reward for lasting through my first MMA fight.

And we begin sparring. I'm working taking angles and trying to land my punches on him. I'm frustrated because the cross is not coming out as the punch I thought it would. Yet, Phil sees me trying.

Then all of a sudden I go to throw a cross and as I do, I do a training habit I picked up last week that is only meant for training. I feel the pain shoot through my scalp like fire burning through the top of my head. My eyes tear up and I'm trying to see, while I hold my hands up to my face.

Phil says, "Jody get down."

I respond, eyes still tearing, "Give me a chance. I got to get use to the pain."

Phil says, "No! No! Get down now."

As I begin to be able to get less teary eyed I say, "*Com'on* give me a chance. I'm fine."

Phil repeats, "No Jody get down now!"

I feel like a wimp. He thinks I'm injured, "Oh, Okay." I drop my hands from my face and go to sit on the ground. Just then a rush of blood as I go to kneel to the ground comes flying through my mouth as I feel a little dizzy at the same time. I see tons of blood everywhere.

I hear Phil, voice less panicked, "Thank God!" He runs off. More blood pours out of my mouth and now nose.

I realize I broke my nose, due to the amount of blood I cannot hold in my mouth. I say, "Oh well, I guess I broke my nose again. I really thought I just had pain, and had to deal with it."

Phil comes rushing back with paper towels, "Thank God. Jody if you didn't bleed at all, I thought I broke your cheek bone. Your face felt like it gave. If that happened, I would have had to bring you to the hospital."

I responded, "Well, I know what I did wrong."

Phil said, "You tilted your head down, as I threw an upper cut."

I responded, "Well yeah. But I was not confident that my rear foot would turn, and it became a bad habit to look down as I threw. I really wanted to throw a good cross."

After we cleaned up the mats, Phil said, "Jody you want to hold pads for Rob?"

I replied, "Yeah, sure. I don't have to be back at work till about nine tonight. I'm good."

Phil sets my nose and then Rob comes over and I work the pads for him. About twenty minutes later as Phil is instructing a couple guys near Rob and I, Phil looks at me. Then he makes a bee-line to me and says, "I have to just fix something."

Phil says, "Hold on a second." Phil resets my nose again. This time it was painful.

After that, Rob says, "What was Phil doing?"

I respond, "Oh, I just broke my nose, like twenty-five minutes ago. Phil broke it. He just set it again."

Rob responded, "You're kidding me."

I reply, "No. Phil and I were sparring. I went to throw my cross and I dipped my head down, due to lack of certainty of my form. Phil threw an upper cut and it landed."

Rob seemed a little shocked. Then we continued to train, until I had to get back to the office to work on a medical doctor.

Afterwards, as a doctor was in to see me for his session. He said, "Phil did a perfect job, I wouldn't be able to tell, if you hadn't said anything."

I responded, "Yeah. It took Phil two tries, but he got it."

At the end of session, I went to wash my hands. Then I saw the bruising start on my face. At this point it was about two hours since the break. I got back to my reception area and the doctor saw me and said, "Now you're starting to bruise."

I replied, "Yeah, I just saw it too. Well, the nose is broken."

We kidded, said 'good-bye'. He departed and I closed up shop.

That night I came home late everyone was sleeping. I checked in on everyone in their beds. Then I went downstairs to check lunchboxes, homework and backpacks. I then made myself a salad, drank water, took some arnica pellets, made a rescue remedy concoction and applied it several times to my face. Then ate half a pineapple for swelling internally and turned on the television, then got sleepy and went to bed.

The next morning, I awoke to Norman kissing me before he was to leave to go to work. He didn't know what I looked like. Norm was leaving for work as usual as the sun had not risen yet. The lights were not on in our bedroom. We said, 'good-bye' as he left.

Our daughters at the time were ages six and eight. Before I knew it, it was time to get them up and ready for school. I gently woke them up, while I made their breakfasts, lunches, my greens, and coffee.

Then with everything set and packed, and children dressed. I called them down for Bible reading and for breakfast. They sat down and as we ate, they looked at me. Both our eight and six year old looked at me and then our eight year began, "Mom, were you fighting last night?"

I responded, "Yes." I thought uh, oh I knew my face was four different colors from eyes down.

Then she added, "With Phil?"

I replied smiling, "Yes."

She continued the questioning, "Does Daddy know?"

I responded, "Not exactly."

Our six year old chimed in, "You know you look a little uh... Psychedelic." As she pointed to her face.

Funny enough it took my husband till about three days later to realize I'd broken my nose. He went and was speaking with one of his teacher friends who'd competed in MMA matches, and described my face to him. Norman was trying to get wise as why my face beneath my eyes were more colorful than usual.

Thursday night he gets home from work and says, "I know what happened to you. I was speaking with Brian, the teacher that's fought MMA in Atlantic City. You have a broken nose."

I respond, "Well, how'd you figure that out. Sure took you a while. The kids knew Tuesday morning."

Chapter Twenty-Four
"The Lamb for Slaughter" (2011)

"You know why they're bringing you out to Oregon?" Rhetorically Phil stated.

I responded, "'Cause they don't have anyone her size?"

Phil replied, "No. They think they can win. They want to make their hometown girl look good."

I respond, "Oh I *ain't gonna* lose."

Phil responds, "You can beat her. I watched her first fight. You beat her, then they'll bring you back out for the 105 pound title fight in Oregon."

I ask, "So when is this?"

Phil responded, "Uh, January 8th,, I think it's a Saturday. They'll pay your way and hotel. I got to get you sparring again."

I reply, "Yeah it's like two weeks since I broke my nose. I could do it. I feel good."

Phil responded, "Okay, let's see, who comes in."

No sooner said then Alex comes in for a night session. We now have just over two weeks till the fight. I knew Phil wanted to see if I was willing to take a shot to the face and if my nose could take the shots. Alex was about six feet one inch tall and a slim 170 pound guy. Phil commandeers Alex to spar with me. Alex always follows instructions. And he has sparred hard with me before. We begin and I'm sparring, fighting like my old self. After about ten minutes. Phil says, "That's' what I needed to see. You were uninhibited. You are not afraid to get punched in the face. That broken nose had no effect on you."

I respond, "Oh, thank God."

Then Phil has Alex and I do drills together to prepare for how I come across the cage and what to attack her with. This is what we do for the next two weeks, with ground fighting and some more sparring.

Soon it is three o'clock in the morning, Friday, January 7th, 2011. I'm picking Phil up from his home and driving us to the airport in Newark. I have a ticket, he has to go on standby. He gets on the flight and we have the same way flying to Utah first, then to Oregon.

We are uncertain of my weight, so we decide not to allow me to eat or drink anything after seven o'clock eastern standard time. The weigh-ins are at around five in the afternoon pacific time.

We arrive in Salt Lake City, Utah at around twelve in the afternoon. Phil let's me have a sip of water as we wait for our flight to board to Oregon. We will land at around two o'clock pacific time. This will give me enough time to weigh myself, run. Weigh myself again after checking into our hotel rooms.

After we get picked up by Darryl the matchmaker outside the airport in Oregon, he's got a lowly pit bull in the back seat. Phil sits in the front of Darryl's truck. I sit in the back seat with the pit bull. He's got all sorts of stuff in the back of his vehicle.

He seems like a nice man. Phil and Darryl chat away. I give the female rescue pit bull treats, wondering where she's been. I can say I'm a little freaked out by her. But then I realize I can't allow that to hurt my energy level and it wouldn't help her get used to me neither. I had no clue how long of a drive this was going to be.

As time passed, we finally get to our hotel. The matchmaker, Darryl says, "I'll pick you up around four. Call me when you feel you're ready then."

Phil responds as we get our gear, "Okay."

As Darryl pulls away, I say to Phil, "I'm dying. I need to know how much I weigh, and I need to go for a little run and shake these legs out."

Phil, responds, "Okay, we have to get checked in."

Then we go to get checked in, they have only one room for us. The promotion didn't give us two different rooms. The place is worn, old and people have all sorts of dogs and such in this hotel. It's about thirty-five dollars a night. It's a hole alright. A real dive. Phil is able to get his own room. They have cable television, coffee pot, and computer accessibility, thank God.

Phil says, "Call me after you get settled. Then I'll give you the scale I brought with me, so we can get your weight."

I reply, "Oh, good. I feel skinny."

Soon enough I call Phil and go to his room and retrieve the scale. I'll go back my room, strip down, weigh myself, call Phil, and give him my weight.
I get back to my room, pray. Strip down and I'm 103.6 pounds. I have to be under 105. I call Phil, "I'm 103.6 Phil, that's before I run."

Phil responds, "That's great, have a little something."

I ask, "How about a quarter of a protein bar and half cup of coffee?"

Phil responds, "That sounds good. You can take in a couple sips of water."

I reply, "Then I'll go for a little run."   We say 'good-bye'.

I have a little coffee and part of protein bar, sip three sips of water. Then get changed, and then I go for about a four mile run. It was my first time in Oregon and I get to run in the state too. It was in a busy area. I found a steak place close by our hotel. I sighted other popular eateries as I ran that would be good for Saturday morning, the morning of the fight.

After I finished my run, I got to my hotel room.
Again, I stripped down and weighed myself. I was now
103.2 pounds. I took a shower, got dressed, then called
Phil and said, "I am now 103.2 pounds I ran about four
miles just before. I'll have another four ounces of
coffee, four ounces of water and a bite of the protein bar.
How's that?"

Phil responds, "Very good. I'll call you after I call
Darryl. He will come and pick us up for the weigh-ins."

I reply, "Okay. Oh, and by the way. A steak place is
two blocks away from our hotel, so I want that tonight.
Okay?"

Phil says, "You got it."

Soon enough albeit Darryl is a little late, he picks us
up to go to weigh-ins. My nerves ebb and flow. I'm still
starving, but know I am on weight. And at this point that
is all that matters.

The place is about two miles from our hotel. I see
other hotels on the way and wonder, '*hmmmm*, had I
known they had a hotel here like this, I would have
asked them for it'.

After we arrive at the site for the weigh-ins, there is
paperwork to be filled out. It is about six o'clock in the
evening pacific time. I've been without a full meal since
Thursday night at seven o'clock, that was at eastern
standard time. Now it was six o'clock in the evening
pacific time, Friday night. I calculated, between
morning grapefruit, grasses, coffee, water and total half a

protein bar I may had 250 calories in about the last twenty-seven hours.

There are delays. They are waiting for fighters, coaches, other people, officials, photographers and the like to be present. They announce there will be food presented after the weigh-ins. I tell Phil, "I need space. I'm feeling uneasy, I need room to breath, and I want to eat in peace. I need steak. And I think we can walk back to our hotel, and the steak place is within a half mile on the same side of the road as our hotel is."

Phil responds, "Yeah. You are right. I'll let Darryl know that you need to walk. And that you have a special place to go eat."

Finally, it's time to weigh-in. I wait for my name to be called. And when it is I strip, fast like never before. I'm thinking '*STEAK!*' My body is breaking down, it's shaking as I strip. I strip down to my skivvies, and as I do I'm throwing my clothing at Phil. I do aim for his lap, but I'm so jittery the clothing is thrown at him. I say, "Sorry Phil." Phil has this blank look on his face. He knows me as to be very conservative and modest.

Then I'm weighed in. I'm 103.3 pounds, even with earrings on. She weighs in less than that. I believe I heard 101.2 pounds. It's a first, an only, and a rarity for me that anyone is less than I am for a fight or ground fight. Then they have us face off for pictures. I'm done.

As fast as I stripped the clothing off I'm now freezing, putting it back on seems clumsy yet almost as fast. I ask Phil, "Can we get going? I'm dying. I need steak."

Phil replies, "Yeah. Let me go let Darryl know we will walk back."

I respond, "Okay." I'm avoiding any talk or eye-contact. I am weak. I need food and mental calm. I need to get fight ready on other levels now.

Phil returns about fifteen minutes later and says, "Okay let's go. We would've had to wait for him till ten o'clock to get a ride back, we need rest and you need to eat what you're use to."

We collect our stuff and get outside into the cold, yet somewhat arid air of a dark Oregon night. It is now near eight o'clock pacific time. We walk about the same slow pace for two miles. Then Phil says, "Let's stop at this store here."

We walk into a convenience store. We both need to get water, and then I see beef jerky in these containers at the counter. There are tongs and little wax paper bags. I'm so hungry, that I need beef before the steak. I say, "Phil, look beef jerky!" I get all excited.

Phil is holding water bottles standing beside me. I then grab the tongs and try holding the wax paper bag open. Only problem is I'm shaking so much I can't get the beef jerky into the wax paper bag. I start to snarl out loud, because I'm getting frustrated.

Phil says, "Let me help you." My hands shaking, I grunt. I became so primitive. I just saw food and wanted to eat it. But I knew I had to bag it and pay for it. My brain was fighting with my hungry stomach. Phil helps me get the beef jerky into the wax paper bag.

Then he says, "I got this." I grunt in gratefulness.

Then as the cashier rings it up, I see all is paid for, and she is ready to hand him back change. While simultaneously I open the bag of beef jerky, and seemingly growl as I overload my mouth with beef jerky. The look on the cashier's face is…well, one of fear or astonishment. I wasn't sure which it was.

I nod my head, mouth now stuffed with jerky where I can't speak or I'll choke. Phil politely thanks the cashier and says 'good-bye'. We exit out the store. I'm trying to say, '*boy I'm hungry*'. However, all you can hear are snarls, as I try to chew, and scarf the jerky down.

Phil remarks, "Well, that was scary."

Finally with only half a mouth full of jerky. I respond, "God, I'm so hungry. I wanted to dive into the beef jerky container, and just eat. Thanks for paying. I got you on dinner."

Phil asked, "Did you see that look on the cashier's face?"

I replied, "Uh. No. What happened?

Phil responded, "You scared her."

I replied, "No way. Get out of here. I did not."

Phil remarked, "Hey, I thought you were scary."

Then as we kid each other. We walk to our hotel and drop the water and other items from the store at Phil's room, then off we walk to the steakhouse a little way up the road. It is now about eight forty or so at night.

We arrive at the steakhouse. Phil is a vegetarian. I'm a beef eater. He orders five baked potatoes. I order thirty ounces of steak and give Phil my baked potato. I order extra green vegetables. Between that and the double salad, I will ingest five servings of green vegetables and the thirty ounces of steak.

We talk as we eat. We hash out points he saw and things I picked up and questions about what her style might be. Before we know it the bill is paid and we are walking back to our respective hotel rooms.

Soon it is Saturday morning, I slept in till eight thirty. I go out for a run at nine o'clock or so. Phil finds a store that carries his favorite bars. I go to a coffee shop, and bakery in the opposite direction, run there and back getting in four miles easily.

We touch base, we talk and then I rest again. I'm back in bed at eleven that morning. I promised my husband I would call him after the fight. It's live-streaming that night, so he can watch it. Norman let's people know. Phil and I decide to walk to and from the event. It is the one thing we can control. We need some control.

Before we know it, it's time. We walk to the place where the event is to be. He has the fight gear on rollers. And the sidewalk is fairly smooth, it is probably under two miles. It is not too bad outside, it's been sunny and not so damp out either. Earlier in the day, I could see the mountains that people were driving to, to ski on as I ran. I saw that they also had cross-country ski areas locally that were in operation. The area was very active.

When we arrived at the event center, it was a bar type place with a very rustic in appearance. They had us come in register, get a medical review done, then go outside and stand outside until they had everything set up. It was getting colder as darkness was about to set in.

Before we stood outside, during the medical check, the young doctor, saw my age. He was a runner. He couldn't believe how old I was. He was so overly cautious, it freaked me out. We were in this cold area of the building. I was freezing. My blood pressure which is usually on the low side was high, according to him.

I asked, "Well, why don't you let me get warm and then take my blood pressure. Because it's usually ninety-eight over sixty-eight."

So he did and sure enough it was normal. Then he added, "Yes, you being cold would affect the blood pressure results."

Then it was a *go*. We were fight number four on the card. Phil wrapped my hands, we had them checked by one of the referees. And of course everyone was finding out my age, and there of course were tilts of heads and such. That, Phil and I expected. We knew this going in.

In one of the first three fights, one of my opponent's teammates was knocked out. Phil turned to me and said,

"That will set the mood. They can't be feeling all that good tonight after that."

I said nothing, for I didn't know how all that worked in fighting. Phil would speak, and I would listen. That's all I knew at this point. Then the time had arrived and the music for my walk out was by *George Thorogood's "Bad to the Bone"*. Big Kyle (Kyle Rigby), gave me the CD with the song on it, so I could bring it to Oregon. Phil thought it was perfect.

And so it played. Since I was '*the lamb for slaughter*', I walked out first. I go through the whole check the body and the mouth-guard thing. And Phil had reminded me, "They expect you to lose. But you're going to win. That's why they paid your way. Just like practice. You know what to do." Phil had said.

He'd later reiterate, "It's not about you. It's about their hometown girl winning. You're just a body." I knew that. However, my fun was the fight itself. Getting to compete in fighting was what drove me. That was my cake. The icing would be the win.

Soon after I was in the cage, my opponent came out during her walk out song. She entered the cage and I heard everyone was for her. The place was packed.

I tried not to look around. I said, "Phil. I got to look at you one more time. You look at me. Now!" My nerves were catching fire.

Phil replied, looking at me, "You're fine. Just like practice."

Then the referee came to both our corners and restated the rules briefly. Then he brought us together to the center of the cage. The referee had us touch gloves at the center. Then he sent us back to our corners. The referee checked with all officials to be ready. It was a *go*. The referee said, "Go!" We went.

Actually I went. I went so fast across the cage, she moved one step and I was all over her like white on rice. I punched she ducked.

I picked her up by her neck. She jumped to guard on me standing up and now holding her head/neck under my left armpit. I begin to walk with her on me like a baby monkey. I cannot hear Phil. He is screaming, "Bring her over here!"

Phil I know he sees me carrying her toward the center of the ring, as I punch her with my right fist. And try choking her with my left arm. I wonder what to do with the body to seal the guillotine completely. So I walk around in a circle punching her, thinking, as Phil is still screaming as well, and her side is calling out orders.

Then I heard one of her corner men say, "Don't worry, she'll get tired."

All of a sudden it was like a car was screeching. I was so insulted. I got pissed and thought, '*Who do they think I am? I never get tired. This little girl has no stamina. No one in this building has ran on a treadmill for twenty-four hours. Damn it! I got the damn North American Women's Twenty-Four Hour Treadmill Record. Screw them! I'll show you tired!*'

Meanwhile as I'm figuring out where to put her. Phil turns to the Oregon official sitting beside him and says,

200

"Wait. That's their plan. Wait till Jody gets tired. They're going to try to tire her out. Well, good luck with that."

Then as I bring her body toward the cage again, while punching her. I'm still carrying her back to her corner. It seemed closest. I then figure, *to thrust my hips up to push her backside into the cage wall. Then it may create space to seal the guillotine tighter, then punch her with upper cuts. It will make her nervous.* So I forge ahead with the plan and it worked. I was able to seal the guillotine. She taps out in just over one and half minutes into the first round. I win!

The referee calls it. I run towards my corner and say, "I think I won. Did I win?!"

Phil looks at me, nods and says, "Yes". I turn.

And then they let Phil into the cage. He hugs me. I respond, "Wow! Did I do good? Did I do what you wanted?"

Phil replied, "Exactly what we practiced. I'm so proud of you."

Then they make it official. I get my hand raised above my head by the referee. As I go to exit the cage after the photo-ops. The MC has a little open-mic with me. Then as I walk back to the staging area, I make eye-contact with the audience. Some people high-fived me. I realized they had announced my age. She, Crystal Jewell was twenty-four years old. She grew up in her

Dad's Dojo. She too had been doing Martial Arts at a young age, since she was around three or four years of age, I was told.

I now re-enter the back staging area, and I can watch the rest of the fights from there or behind the audience. They take off my four ounce gloves and shin guards. The people back stage some stare at me and some come over, and congratulate me. It is though I'm an alien.

Soon my opponent and who appears to be her boyfriend come over to me, and start asking me questions. I'm as old as her parents are, or about that.

She asks, "How come you're so strong?"

I don't know how to answer this, because it is a life-time of answers. I remained silent at first. Then I replied, "Well, I run a lot."

She looked at me dumbfounded.

Then I continued, "…With water-bottles in my hand on runs, and races for years. I didn't have a washer and dryer as a kid. I washed clothes starting at four and half years old in the bath tub with my mother. Wringing out clothes, towels makes you strong. Hanging clothing up on wash-lines helps too."

Her eyes widened, and jaw dropped slightly, "Oh." Her boyfriend just looked at me.

I didn't know how else to explain it. I was confused. Because I began to realize by looking at her physique that she had no calluses. She was handled gently. I was rough and always have been. It was as though she had the freedoms presented to her. I had to find them.

As the night of fighting continued, we enjoyed hanging out for a while, chatting with people and just watching how some fights went. Towards the end, Phil and I were realizing we were going to have to get up at three in the morning to get to the airport and fly back home.

Phil walked over to where I was and asked, "You ready to go?"

I responded, "Yeah. You want to head back now?"

Phil replied, "Yeah. Do you want to walk back?"

I responded, "Absolutely. That's fine with me. I'm feeling hyper. Yet, I need a shower. I feel filthy."

Phil replied, "I'll go find Darryl and tell him we are heading out."

I respond, "Sure. I will wait here."

We re-situated our belongings and then Phil went to find Darryl and the promoter to thank them and let them. Also letting them know we were heading out. As I stood there, people recognized me, and made eye-contact. Some shook my hand, introduced themselves and sometimes chatted with me.

The people, Phil and I found throughout that area of Oregon were very polite. Also at the fights they too marveled that a woman of forty-eight years old was willing to fight a young man's sport. One man, came over to me with a mug of beer in his hand. He began to talk to me. He smiled and asked, "How old are you?"

I replied, "Forty-eight sir."

He shook his head, smiling, and said, "I love it. More power to us. You're helping our generation." We then laughed, and talked more before Phil came back.

As Phil arrived he said, "Okay, you ready?"

I responded, "Yeah." I said good-bye to my new Oregonian friend with the mug of beer, who was quite the gentleman. We high-fived each other as I departed.

Phil said, "Darryl offered to drive us back and to the airport. But I told him that he already had a long weekend. And I told him we would walk back, and then take a cab to the airport."

I responded, "Smart. I'll pay for the cab. It's a long day for Darryl. Walking will feel good." Phil agreed. As we walked through the crowd, some people shook my hand. It was like some kind of family or class reunion. As if I knew all these people. There were so many, I couldn't count. More than at *New Breed* Fights in October 2010. I didn't think I'd get a fight, with an audience that was much bigger than that. Again, it was another amazing experience. The kind you never forget.

As Phil and I walked back about two miles to our hotel, with the gear he had on rollers. We chat. It's pretty late. But I know I won't really sleep. Besides I have phone calls to make. I have to also call, and check work messages. Then take notes on messages from clients as I wait for my third flight.

This will be a long day of travelling ahead, but I need to jump back on family and work items. So I first call home and chat with hubby. I call up my old ultra-running coach Dante in Florida. He loves watching MMA. I call Nina in Michigan. Next it's checking my work week schedule and seeing who called me, and to schedule calling them in between my flights, setting up appointments for the next couple weeks of when people need me.

After cleaning up, phone calls, some coffee and watching some cable television that I don't get at home, I pass out for thirty minutes. I get up and make certain everything is packed. Then I call Phil at the time he wanted me to. He then called the cab.

Before we know it, we are in the cab and being driven to the airport in Oregon. I had three flights to get back home. The first one was to Seattle, the second was to Minnesota, and the last was to Newark, New Jersey airport where I've parked our minivan in long-term parking. Phil is on different flights to get back home.

As Phil sits to my left in the brightly lit Oregon airport, the airport is about half the size of my town Midland Park's Lower Elementary School. Which only holds Pre-K through second grades. I can't sleep. I'm still ramped up. I look over at Phil who stops using his laptop, puts it away and starts to fall asleep. He is sitting up, his left leg is over his right leg as he leans on his left hand and his left elbow. His left elbow is on the arm of the chair he's sleeping in.

I really thought I was hallucinating, when I saw his socks and shoes and pant leg for a second. Without seeing Phil's face, I swear it was a replica of an old next door neighbor, who had passed around January 2004, after he'd moved away just five months before.

The neighbor that Norman and I enjoyed was Al DeMartini, a strapping eighty-three year old man. A man who well into his eighties still could clean his gutters, and help his nephew put a bathtub in. Al and I pulled out mammoth rocks together, one Sunday July 4th, 1998 in our backyard.

After envisioning this, realizing I was still in Oregon and seeing Phil's pant leg and foot, I started to giggle. I thought, *'Oh God. I could never tell Phil that he dressed a little like Al DeMartini.'*

Phil then wakes up, "Huh?"

I respond, "Nothing."

Figure 9. First MMA win in Oregon

Boy Un-honored

The boy un-honored,
As the prince he be.
He needed some caring,
This young man is he.
But when a boy,
Growing into a man.
Is merely destroyed,
Not given a plan.
It is a shame,
The boy-man needs a lift.
To be a real man,
He needs a gift.
The gift is needed,
From a parent you see.
Not usually from female,
It may not be me.
Then I should hope,
A real man presents.
 So boy-man can cope,
Giving life to his essence.

Chapter Twenty-Five
"…I Could Be Your Grandmother"(2011)

This cute, little, *pisher*, who apparently was in ROTC. Smoking cigarettes like a fifteen year old boy shouldn't be doing. Much less anyone else who really wants to out-stamina someone like me, was getting frustrated.

Hec, I was age forty-eight about to be forty-nine that year. And he was fifteen. Albeit he was a good sized kid with a wrestling background. He was about 160 pounds and about five feet eight inches tall. His build was average and he was still growing.

He was doing the one thing Phil said not to do in his gym. Phil would say, "Don't muscle her. It isn't going to work." And well Phil was correct. Yet, many times even the young men would get into bad old habits, perhaps due to other sports they had been partaking in.

Albeit this young fifteen year old was a toughie. I feared if he weren't so into being in ROTC, he'd be in trouble. It's funny, I read people and would keep it to myself. Then one of the other older men or Phil would comment, "Tough little kid, man. He needs this."

Its funny when you work with so many different personalities and there is so much diversity, it brings out the best in you. Why? Because, you have to learn to get along. You need people to train with. To be a fighter, you need variety. This is so you are given spontaneity, with different scenarios of how to maneuver. Many times it can break old habits. Or the things you do that a Grandmaster like Phil will try to say, and teach to you. Yet, it's not breaking the cycle that you're in.

So here was this young fifteen year old boy. Phil had been trying to break his cycle of forcing a submission, as opposed to working in the direction of the submission. It's the difference between flowing with the current of the river and banging your head against a brick wall over and over again. Hey either might work, but what's easier and most likely to get you a quicker, and less painful result on your end? I would say, '*flowing with the current of the river*'.

So one day, it seemed this fifteen year old tough kid decided and was determined he was going to beat me once and for all. He wanted that guillotine. He knew, none of the men ever had gotten me in a guillotine. So this was his heroism, was to get "The Jody" in a guillotine.

This one afternoon, he tried sweeps to get me into that position. Basically he tried everything. Even, as he was given positions of advantage to start. He was so frustrated. Finally, after twenty minutes of his frustration, I stopped him for a second.

I pulled out my mouth-guard, and said, "You know, you seem awfully frustrated. You're a young man. You weigh fifty-five pounds more than me. And you know what? I'm so old. I'm *sooo ollld*. Why *Hec*, I could be your grandmother."

The young man glared at me, probably thinking, '*what is she getting at?*' I looked back and said, "You can't force a rock that won't move. You have to caress it with water. But I'm just an old bag. What do I know? Don't say, 'Oh shit. Say of Wow! It's a science project. Not a problem."

Then Phil commented, "She's right. Don't muscle her. That's why you are frustrated. She will curl up, and become a rock and you won't move her."

Chapter Twenty-Six
"You're The Son, Your Father Always Wanted"
(2011)

It was a Wednesday, March 16th 2011, I'm in Phil's basement gym. I follow him to the bathroom. He's looking for something as I have my questions about possible upcoming fights for me he's been offered. "So how big is the girl?" I asked.

"Well, they're not sure yet. Hey, you remember that girl that lost the 115 title fight in Oregon, when we were there in January?" Phil asked.

"Yeah, the one with the short blonde hair, good-looking kid, talented with sparkles on her eye lids?" I recalled.

"They're considering having you fight her." Phil replied.

"Wow! She's really good." I responded.

"Well, yeah. She hasn't responded. It's just been proposed to me. No commitment on anything yet. You know she's out of Tara LaRosa's camp in Washington State." Phil said.

"That's cool." I responded.

Phil now had gauze and scissors in his hand. I wondered what he was up to. As we stood alone in Phil's basement gym. I asked, "What's that for?"

"We're punching tonight, and I'm going to wrap your left knuckles with gauze. It's your left hand right?" He asked.

"Oh yeah. I guess it's when I punched your elbow last week. That was nasty. Why didn't I see that while we were sparring? What was I doing?" I asked

Phil responded, "I blocked as you threw and you were squared and not balanced when you threw."

Phil walked over to the Southeast corner of the gym and sat down. I sat down and reached out my left hand for him to wrap the gauze padding onto the broken knuckles of my left hand. Phil began to wrap the hand, placing gauze on the broken knuckles.

Phil finishes up wrapping both hands, the left one padded with gauze on the knuckles, the right hand with my red wrap. Then Phil helped me put my four ounce MMA Men's large gloves on. As he does he says, "You know. You are the son your father always wanted."

I responded, "Really?"

Phil nods, "Yep. Look what you do and how you do it. Any father would want a son like you."

"Oh, cause of what I do?" I asked.

"Yes. But also your attitude." Phil replied.

It was a Wednesday night, at nine. It was my usual
private lesson, day and time with Phil. Then we would
begin the thirty minutes of punching.

Phil would work it in such a way where I would punch
jab, crosses for ten minutes straight, with proper stance
and structure. After every punch my hands were to be
back on my face, especially as the other hand released
the punch, or else he'd comment as soon as I slacked.

Phil would don a belly pad that was black, old, and
leathery. He'd lean into my punches. Move and make
me move, keeping proper structure. Then after a ten
minute round of punching, Phil would give me a one
minute rest.

Phil would then have me do another ten minutes of
punching only this time throwing all hooks. All the
hooks were meant as body shots. Then he'd allow
another one minute rest. Then have me do another round
with ten minutes of punching. Yet again, a change in the
type of punches he wanted. This last ten minute round
would be all upper cuts.

As Phil and I would proceed with each ten minute
round of punching, Phil would ask, wondering
something about me, "How do you count punches?"

I responded as I punched, "676..." and growl...
"Cause....I.... Count in....702... fours..."

The round bell soon rings. I say, "816 hooks."

During this private session, one of Phil's Pros walked in that night. It was Mark. Mark was a very talented wrestler. When it came to fighting that boyish look, when he wore his glasses made him look like a third year student at MIT. So much so, many people would never have guessed that he'd fought Frankie Edgar in Atlantic City just years before.

He sat outside the cage on one of the white plastic chairs watching us. Had Phil not said, "Hello" to Mark, I would've never noticed. I'm an assembly line kind of worker. Just tell me what to do and I will do it. I will remain fully focused until you tell me to stop. I'm on a mission. And so I apply whatever I have to give of myself to get there.

I was on my second round when Mark walked in. During the one minute rest Mark said, "I can't believe what she's doing. That's crazy."

Phil responds, "Mark, Jody does three ten minute rounds of punching with one minute rest every week. She needs a ten minute round fight. That would be a good fight for her. My only wonder is, 'how does she count as she does this'."

I respond, "Rainman goes to Pride?"

Unknown to anyone, I figured that me focusing on counting helps me remember the mission is about the punching, not the pain.

My right hand would bleed, cuts on my knuckles as we proceeded this way on a variety of Wednesday nights for the first thirty-two minutes of our session. By now, I'd be in his basement gym five days a week. This regiment now had began just two years before.

Chapter Twenty-Seven
Birdies or Stars? (2011)

It was late spring 2011, the sun shone through the South windows of Phil's basement gym. The sun seemingly was powerful enough to warm up the red mats that lined the floor. The caged fencing was wrapped around the majority of the walls of the basement room. Eventually the caged fencing was facing nearly all four directions of a compass in the room.

It was a clear, sunny, Thursday lunch-time class at Phil's. Two men were in the back of the basement gym practicing, working pads. I'd just got done working some ground for the first part of class. Then before I know it Phil puts up a rope to denote the fourth side of a caged ring to spar in at the front of the gym. The side towards the east and the entrance to the gym, the west side Phil ropes in when sparring in the front of the room.

As Phil is putting up the rope, Leif walks in. Leif is about 5'10" and about 160 pounds or so. Then Steve walks in. Steve is about 5'10" as well, and a bit huskier a thick 182 pounds give or take a pound. Steve wants to do stand-up. I need sparring practice. I need stand up. I'm really itching to work my stand-up.

I liked working with Steve in stand up. I always learned a lot from Leif when we worked ground together. Leif is super fast on the ground. Leif was wrestling by age fourteen. However, Leif's ability didn't stop there, his punches were scary. Leif was a Golden Gloves Boxing Champion during his mid-thirties. Leif had just turned forty, that May. Leif was a super guy.

217

He and his wife had no children. However, they were a hard working couple, who rescued pit-bulls.

As Phil finished wrapping my left hand knuckles with gauze, I warmed up a little. Then Phil has me do a little ground work. Then Phil decides after that, to have me do some stand-up as well, keeping with our four ounce gloves on. Upon Steve's arrival Phil asks, "You up, you down?"

Steve replies, "Oh, I'll do up."

Phil says, "Okay. You three will do a round robin of stand up." As Phil points to Steve, Leif and myself.

I asked, "Who's to go first?"

I really was disappointed when Phil responded, "Leif and Steve first."

I wonder how many rounds they're going to be able to last, before I get a chance to spar. I hope to I get to spar Steve first, Leif is faster. I need to warm-up on Steve before going with Leif. Although both excellent. Leif is scarier.

Also they both will give me a feel what they may throw consistently this day, and what their movement will be like, as well. I knew Leif had great cardio. Steve is the question mark on cardio. He's been doing much coaching of his daughter's athletic team sports.

First round has passed. We decide to do two rounds on and then switch going two rounds on and then switch one in again. Steve looks a little tired, but not totally wiped. Besides he has a minute to recover and appears to do so.

The second round bell rings, Steve and Leif go at it. About a minute into it, all of a sudden Leif lands a hook square on Steve's jaw line. Steve's hands drop. Steve's body goes to the ground. Phil runs over and the gym stops. Steve is awake but got knocked silly. I walk over and ask, "How is he?"

Phil says, "Steve is okay."

I look down at Steve and ask, "Birdies or Stars?"

Steve responds, "Both."

Then Phil says, "Okay, Steve rest. You're done for the day. Jody go with Leif."

Okay, great. Now I'm really scared. I pray and whisper to myself, *'Cover up. Tuck your chin in'.* The round bell rings. We begin sparring. I decide I'll take the hellacious hits from Leif to the body rather than the head and hold my hands tight to my face. This is to shield with the movement of my arms to block the sides of my head, by moving my hands back as if to grab my own ear.

The first round with Leif, I survive. Second round bell rings, we begin to spar. I'm trying to get into his space to jam his punches and inhibit Leif's ability to throw a hook to my head or a cross straight down the pike. Which in turn would push my head back, and assist in clearing my hands from my face for him to throw a hook or an upper cut. I constantly had to work on crowding Leif's striking angles.

Before I know it, I survive five rounds with Leif. Then class has ended. Leif also had to leave early, lucky for me.

Chapter Twenty-Eight
Offers Come and Go (2011)

From February on forward till near end of August 2011, Phil gets offers of people wanting me on their show to fight. Phil would call me up and say, "You want to fight this weekend?"

I would respond, "Yeah, sure. I just got to check with Norman and the kids. I'll call Norman."

Phil calling me back an hour later then said, "It's in Kentucky."

I replied, "I just called Norman he said he's 'good with it. Go do'."

Phil responded, "Okay, your medicals are still good. They have to get the records from the Athletic Commission of the State of New Jersey. They have to have in the next twenty-four hours."

I replied, "So what do I do?"

Phil responded, "Nothing. It's if, the State office has the time to send the paperwork over to Kentucky."

We wait and the next day fight is called off. Then we got an offer for a fight in Oregon again, but not the one they promised for a title, after I defeated Crystal Jewell. It's at a higher weight-class., I told Phil "I'll take it anyway." Then the girl who was a lot more experienced than I (her record 8-2-0). She said, she felt that her experience would make it an unfair fight. So she doesn't want the fight against me. We were offered two other fights, one in Kansas and Ohio. Between February 2011 and April 2011, all four fights fell through. This would happen where fights would fall through out of nearly one hundred offers thus far from 2010 through 2016. Six of the nearly one hundred fights offered I'd had to turn down for a variety of reasons (two were illness, one was injury, one was financial, and two were due to death and illness of family members). And so life happens.

I asked Phil, "Why is this happening?"

He replied, "They find out your age and the girl wants to win. So they accept it, because they are desperate, but also think no way could they lose and then they watch the Sazoff and Jewell fight and realize, maybe they could lose. Then they sometimes think that if they win or lose they lose regardless because of your age."

I asked, "So who thinks like that? And why?"

Phil replies, "Jody they are there to win. Not to fight. They only want to win. I don't' get it either."

Then we get another offer to fight in *New Breed* in June 2011 in Atlantic City. First the Budo-Fights title winner at 105 pounds that I was supposed to fight, I call her 'Cookie-Puss'. Oh yeah, I have nicknames for the people I'm supposed to fight. Pretty-Puss was from Michigan. Pretty-Puss said 'no', twice, after saying 'yes'. There was Whiney-Puss, The Brat, Bean-Pole, Gorilla Girl, Poser-chick, Butterball, Ketchup, Skittish, Pinkalicious, etc... Yes, I had and have made up names for many of my competitors.

So after Cookie-Puss pulled out, we had a girl from Florida said, 'yes'. Then two weeks later said 'no'. Then a girl from Georgia said 'yes', but didn't have all her medicals done in time. So we decided let's ask Sazoff for a rematch. She will want it, and it will sell tickets.

People told me they wanted a rematch. Sazoff had all medicals except needed a new blood serum pregnancy test. It had to be in by four thirty in the afternoon the Wednesday before the Saturday night fights. She couldn't get the results in till Thursday morning from the doctor. So the Athletic Commission bagged the fight.

I went to train Friday night, knowing I didn't have a fight the next night. Phil was yelling at Peter to pass my guard. Peter was scheduled for a grappling tournament at the end of June. We had about four or five guys training for that.

On the fight card Saturday, in Atlantic City we did have three fighters on the card. However, since they bagged mine, we now had two fighters on the card. I promised Phil and Josh that I would be there to help out, even though I didn't have my fight.

Josh really did want me there. As the first half hour of the class on Friday night progressed, Phil was pressuring Peter more and more to pass my guard. Peter was having a tough time. Then it happened. Peter did what he was supposed to do. However, my foot got stuck on his clothing at the same time which in turn my left knee got twisted. The left lateral portion of my left ankle and lower leg were facing the left side of my face and my femur was perpendicular. Peter landed all of his 190 pounds down twisting the knee perpendicular to the position a hinge joint like the knee isn't supposed to be able to be in. I screamed. Pain shot through me. Phil saw it. We heard it. Peter did back off super-fast. I said, "Phil just pull the knee pad off." My whole body was shaking. "Just pull if off. Tell me I'm okay. If you pull off the knee pad and touch it. I'm okay." Phil, did so. Phil got my knee pad off, pulled down to my ankle and touched the knee. I said, "Just stand me up. I think. Could you get me something?"

Phil responded, "What do you want?"

I replied, "I have a concoction in my pocketbook. The car keys are in my shoe behind the fencing at the cage entrance."

Phil runs, gets my keys, goes to my minivan, and then fetches my pocketbook. Phil comes through the cage with my pocketbook. Meanwhile someone gets me an ice pack. I get up within a minute, and attempt to walk. I think to myself, '*I must pretend it's just a shock to my system. I'm not fully injured, just tweaked.*' I can see Peter feels awful. Only it's not anyone's fault. I keep trying to reassure Peter that it's okay.

I take out the items to make the concoction to get the area from becoming more traumatized. I then take the ice pack off and work my concoction in. I do this on my own for ten minutes. I tell Phil and the guys it is okay.

Peter still looks traumatized. I say, "Hey Pete. I need you to just help me here, okay?"

He responds, "What do you want me to do.?"

Laying on my back, I reply, "Here work the adductors like this." I show Peter the direction. Then I put the concoction on it, and he works it in more. Soon, it actually feels better. I tell Peter, "Okay, now go train." I'll work a bunch on the knee. Big Kyle comes by me and talks a little to me. Phil looks over. He thinks I'm wrecked. But I won't accept that. You never know what a little prayer will do.

I continue to work on my knee, and have Peter work the adductor a little bit before class ends. Then I slowly get to my minivan and tell Phil as I leave, "See you tomorrow in Atlantic City. Don't worry I'll be there. I promised Josh and I don't want to disappoint him."

The next morning is cloudy and damp. Josh had gotten a Rabbi to bless the cage down in Atlantic City before the fights begin, earlier in the day. Josh is an Orthodox Jewish young man. He can't use electronics before sundown, and therefore couldn't weigh in till about twenty-seven minutes before his fight after nine o'clock that night.

As I drive down to Atlantic City the next morning, I have a peg-leg. My left knee hurts. The three hours in my minivan alone, I rub a special homeopathic formula on my left knee. I do this as I drive, and pray for it as well. The whole three hours I did ten applications. I was determined to be there for Phil, and the guys. And I needed to look as natural as possible.

When I got down there, Phil was shocked that I made it down. I hobbled a bit with a peg-leg, told him I was fine. "Movement is good for healing." I told Phil. "What do you need me to do?" I asked him.

Phil said, "Okay, babysit Josh. He can't weigh in till about nine o'clock tonight." I realized that was going to be tough we had about eight more hours to go. I met Josh's friends who were orthodox and kept him on his religion. This was very important. I had to make certain nothing would be in violation of his religion. Phil went looking for an old-fashioned medical scale with no batteries or anything electrical included. It had to be this way, for Saturday was his Sabbath.

I let Josh eat five cashews, and a quarter of a pomegranate. Then I stopped him. Then Phil switched me to taking Rashid to eat with a friend of his. Rashid got to weigh in early when regular weigh-ins were supposed to occur.

So as Rashid and one of his friends, and his son went to the eating area, I made certain no one came near us. I wanted no issue. I stood by as he ate and eye-scanned the area. Then looked at Rashid's plate and asked, "More?" Rashid was going to get up. I wouldn't let him. I'd do what he needed, I was his watch and his legs. Rashid told me what he needed and I fetched it.

After we got done eating I had to make certain Rashid got back up to where the *rules* meeting was and to where Phil would be. We were nearly there. I guarded the bathroom when he went in. I wanted nothing to disturb Rashid on my watch. Phil wanted me to keep trouble away. I was as invested in Rashid as I was in Josh.

Finally, Rashid and I were walking alone. As we walked on the floor just doors away from where Phil was, one of the hotel room doors was ajar. A few girl voices were heard. Rashid, this charismatic, handsome, young African-American man, a heavy-weight fighter with a somewhat suave personality, takes one step past the door. I see a big smile on his face. Before I can grab him. Rashid then takes an about-face one step back and to left, and pokes his head in these ladies' hotel room, while they are apparently getting dressed. I thinking *'Oh God. Phil is going to kill me.'*

He says, "Hello ladies."

They respond almost in unison, "Hi." As they giggle together. It sounds like three of four girls.

Rashid then asks, "I'll see you ladies after my fight."

They comment in a positive way. Giggling and laughing. I felt like yelling, *'Damn it Rashid. Get over here.'* But I refrained. Within thirty seconds Rashid was back to my left smiling as we walked four more hotel room doors to a conference room area, where Phil was sitting.
I came in behind Rashid and looked at Phil, "You got him?"

Phil replies, "Yeah." Then he asks Rashid, "Where's your mouth-guard?"

Rashid lights up, "Oh damn. I don't think I got one."

I respond, "I always carry two. Not formed yet."

Phil replies as he sees me go to my pocketbook, "Oh good. I can see you now, as someone tries to mug you, you saying, 'Hold on. I just have to put my mouth-guard in. Now try and mug me.'"

I respond, "Y*ep*, that would be me."

Soon enough it was time for Josh to weigh-in. I awaited the time the Rabbi said when Josh would not violate the Sabbath for his weigh-in. Josh wanted to eat. I kept track of the last minutes and held onto the scale. Then came the nod and I checked the time. Now Josh was safe to weigh-in.

He was spot on weight. Then before we knew it Josh, Phil and I were going down to the where the fights were taking place. We could have three people in Josh's corner. A former coach was to be in his corner with Phil and I. On our way down, Josh wanted to eat in the elevator, this was twenty minutes before his fight. I held his food. As I went to let him eat, I didn't want one violation and Josh heard me start the Blessing of the Bread in Hebrew as we were in the elevator. *'Phewwwwe!'* I thought.

Then before we all knew it, it was fight time. Josh was ready. Phil handed me his watch to keep time and tell Phil every thirty seconds on time. That night Rashid lost because he didn't listen to Phil. His cardio was off. Rashid was very down.

That night Rashid lost to a decision. Josh won. I got to meet Josh's sister and mother. As people collected their things from the area where we left our belongings, Phil said to me, "I can't believe you made it. You look worn."

I replied, "Well, I promised. I'll be good."

Phil said, "Even Scott said you didn't look good. Thank you Jody."

I responded, "No problem. See you Monday."

On Monday I got in to see my chiropractor. She checked my knee before I had to get into work. After I explained what happened, she checked the left knee and said, "Well, you are really lucky. It's a sprain. But I don't think you'll be running for about six weeks." She told me to ice more and keep doing the salves I was already using.

I saw Phil Monday night and did pad work. I told him what my chiropractor said. Phil said, "I have to tell you I thought for sure it was worse. How do you feel?"

I replied, "Really not too bad. I think I'll be running in less than a month. That's my feeling."

Then after four days had passed, it was now Tuesday. I just had an urge to run. I decided to run for no more than two miles and very slowly and make certain I wasn't limping. It took me twenty minutes of pain throughout my left leg, yet I accomplished two miles.

Then called Phil and said, "Hey, you're not going to believe this no limping, just tons of pain. I ran a very slow two miler this morning before work."

Phil replied, "Wow, Jody that's amazing. I wouldn't have expected that."

I said, "See you Wednesday night. I'm good."

It took me approximately three weeks to get back to a normal pattern of running eighty miles a week. And at the same time we got another offer from Michigan. We were all set to drive up there on a Thursday morning,
The 115 pound fight was set for Saturday, it was the third week in July, my left leg felt pretty good. So the Monday going into the fight week, Phil went to get finality on hotel, food and gas money they would pay us. The promoter all of a sudden couldn't get a hold of my opponent or their coaches.

By Wednesday night, the promoter couldn't get an answer, so he drove to the gym that the coach and girl trained out of. The coaches' response, "No way am I letting my girl fight that animal."

Phil then was contacted right before I came in for my private session Wednesday night at nine o'clock. And gave me the news. I said, "They think I'm an animal? What the *hec*? She's taller, bigger, and younger than I am. And probably more experienced than I. I have to be an animal."

Phil was livid to say the least, "All's they had to say was 'no', like last week after they saw a film of yours."

It was the second time out of Michigan that year we heard the word, 'no' from a fight camp. Then the well seemed dry. I told Phil I'm going on vacation with the family the third week in August. Don't worry, I'll stay in shape."

Soon enough, I was on vacation with my family. I ran ten to fifteen miles a day in the woods of New Hampshire. I took the kids fishing as Norman relaxed by the pool. There was a river you could fish and swim in close by. And then there was the pool. We had our own little cottage which was also an efficiency. About the fifth night we were there, a Wednesday night my cell phone rings, it's Phil.
I answer, "Hello."

"It's Phil." Phil responds. He continues, "Is this a good time?"

I replied, "Yeah, sure. What's up?"

Phil says, "I got a possible fight at 110 pounds in Missouri, do you want..." Phil hasn't finished his sentence.

I responded, "I'll take it."

Phil says, "Hey but wait you don't even know the details."

I replied, "I need it. I'll check with Norman. But I'd like it."

Phil gives me the details. It is Saturday, September 10th in Missouri, whole way paid. I'm happy. I tell him, "Tell them 'yes', I'll take it."

We say our good-byes. I let my husband know and he's cool with it. That night, we slept soundly. However, when I woke up, my left ribs were popped out. They were dislocated. And they hurt. They had been dislocated like this since end of 2009. Phil had been taping my ribs every day since then, as soon as I walked into the gym. And I wanted this fight. So I prayed as I ran the remaining days and just did easy drills, no sit-ups. It slowly went back in over the next four days, so by the time I got home I had pain, yet the ribs didn't look or feel dislocated.

Before I know it Labor Day passes and the school starts for my husband and our children. Phil gets another offer for October 1st for a fight at 105 pounds for me in Chicago. I take that one too. So now I have two fights within three weeks of each other.

And then before we know it, it's time to fly to Missouri. There were flight issues. Yet somehow, we fly out there, even after the airlines tells me my ticket is not correct. Something got screwed up.

However, we make it in time for weigh-ins, and medicals the day before the fight. I weigh in at 109 pounds. She's about five feet eight inches tall. Rail thin. Then the medicals, the rib still ached, but it was in. And no one knew it, besides Norman who was back home in New Jersey. So during my medicals this new young female doctor is doing my exam. She goes to touch my ribs. I pull back, and giggle. She giggled out of embarrassment, I guess. Hey, she tickled me. Then I realized, '*Wow. I'm out of pain. What luck?*' Off we go back to the hotel and I go for a run before we go out to eat.

Soon it is fight morning, I get out for a four mile run, in another state I've never been to. The trees were pretty, and the landscape was undulating more than I pictured. Phil takes me for coffee, scones, and picking up some protein bars and water as well.

Missouri had wicked storm clouds both in the evening and the day of the fight. The fight's promotion are Pro-Am, *Shark Fights* and *Blue Corner* are working the promotion together. So we'd be in rooms among the pro-MMA fighters as well.

As time passed and we went through the routine of Phil wrapping my hands, my hands getting checked. The rules meeting, last minute medical checks, soon enough we were being escorted to go for the walk out. My walk out song I wanted was the original, "*American Woman*" by the *Guess Who*. I didn't hear it play, I was so ready we had had so many turn-downs, about fifteen to twenty in under a year. And here it was eight months, and one week from my last MMA fight. I feared ring rust.

Before I knew it, I was in the cage, waiting for my opponent Nadia Nixon. She towered over me. Yet I saw that neck. I knew she was bigger and she had really good ground technique. It's what I'd been finding out about the smaller women's weight-class, that most had good ground games.

Then after we were announced, and in our respective corners, the referee brings us to the center, to touch gloves there and then to go back to our respective corners till the referee tells us to 'go'.

I get back to my corner and Phil is sitting there on the other side of the cage and he says, "Jody, just like practice." Then he mouths the words, '*snap that head down.*' I nod.

The referee then sees if the officials are ready and then 'go'. I come in across the cage as quickly as possible and start swinging. She is punching back. Then before I know it we are on the ground. Then she gets mount and is pounding me, I'm punching up in between her punches. I'm fighting from my back. She is landing. I see the referee checking me. As I'm getting punched, I calmly say, "I'm fine."

Soon the first round is over. I know she's got that round in the books. The fight doctor is ready to come into the cage to check on me. Phil asks, "What are you laughing about?"

I respond, "Oh man…" I giggle more. "Yeah, she got that one."

The doctor is ready to check me. Then he shakes his head and waves it off and goes back to his official seating outside the cage. He sees I'm fine. Phil says,

"She can't match your energy. She will fade in her punches."

Soon enough the second round is upon us. The referee gives the go ahead. And again I come across as fast as I can with structure to land my punches. I chase her a little bit, trying to land punches.

Then again we are on the ground, I'm trying to block her from swinging her hips and legs around and over me to submit me with an arm-bar. I prevent it for a while and then I make a mistake, I lift my body-weight up and she is able to sweep me into her mount and more ground and pound.

Again, I tell the referee, "I'm fine." As she punches me on the ground. I'm just waiting out this part of the storm. And then again before we know it the sound of the end of round two comes.

I get up, I realize I may have lost that round, however, she did weaken about a minute into it. Her punches were getting less and they weren't landing as hard. And as I get back to my corner, Phil reaffirms my thinking, "Jody, the first half of that round was hers. You did good though. Her punches began to really weaken within the first minute of that round. You're doing good."

I feel warmed-up now. I'm in the game. I think, *'I somehow got to nail her. How am I going to get that neck?'* Phil has also implied, that I really have to either knock her out or submit her at this point. This is her town, not mine.

I get up off the stool pretty quick and she is still seated. She is tired. I think, *'Maybe I got this thing.'* Then the referee begins the third and final round. Again,

I go in for the attack. She's weaker. She is fighting differently. She's now using her kicks to the body. I eat the kicks to the body, and walk forward. I do this as I attempt to land punches. The first bunch of kicks I take mostly to my left ribs. I can see it in her eyes. She's wondering, *'why is this not stopping her?'*

After many kicks, and I felt one. So I covered my left side a slight bit, without her seeing that maybe I felt it. During the third round, she brings me to the ground again. Only this time I'm able to apply what Phil is beginning to teach me in training about popping up out of guard. And then making the other person have to stand up, and fight standing with me.

She is now weak, I can feel it as I'm in her guard. I pop up to the standing position bringing myself nearly to the middle of the cage, when she was nearly comfortable resting on her back near the cage fencing. I look at her laying on her back.

She expects me to come over and play her game. I take my right index finger, looking at her I wiggle my right index finger back and forth and call to her, *"Com'on* get up."

I then hear the crowd, *"Oooooooohhhhh."* I almost laughed.

The referee looks over at her and commands her to get up and fight. She's none too happy. I hear a huff and grunt of unhappiness from her, as she gets up. Then we continue fighting and before we know it the third and final round is over.

We thank each other, and hug. Our corners come over hug, shake hands, and her coach says to me, "That was amazing? How old are you again?"

I respond with a smile, "I'll be forty-nine next month sir. Thank you."

He held my hand, smiled and shook his head, "Wow!"

Then the referee calls us to the center of the cage and they announce the winner. I lose to a decision.

We talk and take pictures afterwards. The doctor looks at me, he shakes his head. He's younger than I am. I think I just blew his mind. But I still don't really get it.

Then Phil and I talk to Nadia and another woman who was the matchmaker, who was pregnant at the time. She fights as well. She also had fought Nadia and that came down to a decision as well. The matchmaker/fighter was my height. Then Phil and I went back to the staging area to get my gloves returned. As we did this, and I called Norman to let him know how I was and how I did. I felt bad that I lost. Phil also spoke with Norman as well.

Then one of the men who was a well-known pro MMA fighter there said to me, "I cannot believe those kicks you took. They didn't even bother you."

I responded, "Yeah?"

The pro says, "I've never ever seen anyone do that. That was amazing. You're tough."

I responded, "Awe, thanks. Cool."

He repeated, "Yeah. That was something."

After all phone calling and getting my wraps off my hands, we went back out to watch some of the fights that were still going on. I looked at Phil and asked, "Hey I think my eyeballs hurt."

Phil says, "You look okay."

I reply, "Well, it's when I move them like this." And show him.

Phil says, "You probably have corneal abrasions. She was scraping those punches when she had mount."
So before we got going back to the hotel, we got me eye drops and that helped. I had also gotten dirt in them, being on the cage floor so much.
Days later I found out that I had corneal abrasions in both eyes, by the sixth day it calmed down a lot. I wasn't feeling right so I went to another doctor and he said, "You got to take it easy for about a week." I had a full week of work. And unknown to me, because I was not feeling good, had to work and get back into the swing of things children, husband, house, meal planning for the week, and take care of my health on top of that.
The day one of my doctors wanted to do a procedure on me. I told him, "I have too much to do." However, I

could bypass any drugs or anesthetics. It's really because of my mind and my thinking. Then he ordered me to not run, and to rest till Monday September 19th, 2011.

I drove home from the procedure, exhausted, yet happy that I took care of business. I had gotten up at four 'clock in the morning to run, knowing he might not let me do any kind of exercise at all for a little bit. Which was a good guess on my part, even though he warned me, 'we *would have to do more on Wednesday*'.

I scheduled it around work, and had it so I could go back to work only lightly working on people. I would not lift anything and had our babysitter retrieve the children from school. This time he would let me go for a run the day after the second procedure. Yet, I told him, "Listen I have fight on October 1st, can I fight then?"

His first answer was, "You should be fine by then." However, two things happened one on Monday September 19th, 2011, and the other on Wednesday, September 21st. First Phil had just found out on Monday that Leif Mickens died Saturday, September 17th 2011 in a car accident while coming home from working in Boston, late at night. The wake was Wednesday night. Then after having the second procedure done, which was in between two work loads of people, and nine hours of work. The doctor then told me, he had to see me in a week. I was not yet out of the woods. Yet, the doctor still assured me I'd be fine for the October 1st fight in Chicago, which Phil and I wanted desperately to have me fight.

After Leif's wake Wednesday night, the gym didn't feel the same. I was a little down, as were many of the guys in the gym. I couldn't imagine what it was like to be Phil. Then the next downer, the surgeon said, "You're fine but after checking. I really want to do one more."

I replied, "You assured me this was going to be okay. I now have to let my coach know. Which then the other people involved will be upset. I'm certain about that. Why didn't you even tell me this a week ago?"

He replied, "Because I had to wait and see."

I was so pissed. I almost walked out of the surgical area. I'd been doing this procedure stuff with no assistance, going back to work, and going about my business on the last one.

After the procedure, I was advised I had to cancel the fight. Now I had to go tell Phil. I can't remember who screamed at him. But it wasn't pretty. And then as a fighter you are always reminded, *'no one but the fight trainer really cares about their fighter but them'*.

I then went to Phil's holistic healer and asked him his opinion. He actually wanted me to wait a total of eight weeks before hard sparring or getting punched again. He had a clue.

He knew Phil and he trained with Phil for years. So I abide. I could roll, just carefully. I worked on my stand up without sparring. I healed. A rough month indeed…The passing of Leif Mickens was brutal.

Many Brothers I Have...

What is a brother?
Some may ask.
It is another,
Willing to take a task.

The task they take,
Not transparent or fake.
It adds to our life,
And may lower strife.

They are not relation,
No Nation connection.
But solid as a man,
They take on a stand.

They'll hold to their ground,
Even taking a pound.
They'll leave nothing behind,
Get you out of a bind.

If you ask they tell,
Their egos don't swell.
They'll give you the truth,
Even if uncouth.

Loyalty not swayed,
Even if dismayed.
And in the end,
Their hearts will not bend.

They'll give their best,
So that you may rest.
As you remain friend,
Your hearts will mend.

Figure 10. What a Bunch...Coach Phil, Rashid, Antonio pointing to Jody's head, Bruno and Josh. Five of us fought on the same card in Virginia January 2012

Chapter Twenty-Nine
Happy Mother's Day (2012)

What would a woman, especially a mother want for the Friday night before Mother's Day? Sleep, so one would think. Me? A great sparring match or perhaps a MMA or Boxing match.

So here we were the Friday before Mother's Day 2012. I come into the gym that evening for the seven o'clock class. I do some pad work and then Phil says, "This is a kid that Tim knows. He wants to spar, but has never fought or anything. He doesn't have a mouth-guard. You want to go light with him?"

I respond, "Yeah. Sure. I'll go ten percent to the head and about forty-five percent to the body, okay?" I look at the kid and Phil.

I think, '*No experience. Kid says he's 145 pounds, go light. No problem.*' I do some light work with him, before we spar lightly.

Then I ask, "Are you ready to spar?"

He responds, "Yes."

I go real light, not wanting to scare, hurt or bruise him in anyway. Phil is in the front of the basement gym working with guys who are sparring. Then after about a minute, he throws a combination that only someone who was well-trained throws. I get punched in the face, kicked in the crotch. I warn him, "Kicks to the crotch are illegal in MMA, and we are not in Burma where they are legal." He nods. I continue, "Okay, let's start again."

Then about thirty seconds into the 'light' sparring I'm still maintaining what I promised. Again, he lands the same wicked combination on me and nailing me in the crotch. Okay I think, *'Now I want to kick his ass'.* I verbally remind him as I grab him subduing him and putting him in a choke hold. He taps.

We start again, I remind him. Again, he throws this combination and again I receive a crotch kick. Now I know my crotch area is definitely damaged. I repeat the punch, grab and guillotine to choke him and he taps again.

This went on with him with different combinations, and getting kicked in the crotch, me subduing him, choking him and he tapping out ten times. At the end of the night, as everyone was saying *'good-bye'*, the kid says, "You be in Monday night?"

I respond, "Yes. You want to spar again? Bring a mouth-guard this time, please."

Everyone exits except me. I ask Phil, "Everyone is gone?"

Phil says, "Yes, What's wrong?"

I lose it, "What's wrong? Do you hate me? What the Fuck was that?" I lean against the white wall across from the boxing ring. The pain is increasing in my crotch. I'm practically sliding my rump to the floor, the pain is increasing.

Phil asks, "What happened?"

I replied, "That kid. He knows stuff. He's got experience and how. Who sent him in here? How old is he?"

Phil shocked responded, "Tim sent him here. He's nineteen."

I say, "Phil he's 160 pounds, not 145. He has experience and how! He nailed me in the crotch ten times. I'm in pain, man!"

Phil saw me curling up against the wall in pain. He runs and gets me an ice pack for my crotch. Phil comes back with an ice pack. I stuff it in my pants. Phil, "He threw combinations that only our guys would throw who are experienced. This kid lied. Big time!"

Phil asked, "You know if he's going to come back?"

I replied, "Oh yeah. He's coming back Monday night at seven o'clock and wants to spar with me, again. You check. You make sure this kid is nineteen."

Phil said, "Jody I really had no clue. I'll call Tim, he knows him."

Then I get changed and I leave, "See you tomorrow morning Phil."

That night I can't sleep I'm in throbbing pain in bed. I'm in kill mode in the morning. I go for a very painful run and get cleaned up, then saying *good-bye* to hubby, and children and to Phil's I go. I come in and Phil is speaking with Derek and Peter.

Derek says, "You want me to take care of him for you."

I said, "No. It's mine. Phil, come here. Come see the damage."

Phil follows me, "What's up?"

To not get too personal, due to my modesty, I left up my tights that are short left pant leg just three inches below my groin area. The blood is from my crotch and you can see bleeding all the way to the inside of the left knee.

Phil remarks, "Oh man."

I reply, "So I'm pissed. I got no sleep last night from having too much pain. I 'm pissed. Let me think about this."

After class, we say our '*good-byes*' and I head off for the rest of my weekend with the family. Monday morning after taking care of the children in the morning,

I decide to gut it through a fifteen miler, regardless of the groin and crotch pain that is brutal with every step.

About ten kilometers (six point two miles) into the run, the pain in the crotch area is horrid. I have my cell phone on me for the children, but I am way angry, and needed to let Phil know. I call. Phil answers, "Hello."

I say, "Phil its Jody. I'm running. I'm in pain in the crotch. It's disrupting my life and I'm way pissed. Actually I'm enraged."

Phil responds, "Uh what do you want?"

I reply, "You check that kid's I.D., then if he is not a minor. Hand him to me. Let me do what I need to do."

Phil says, "You sure?"

I reply, "You give me that little *fuck'r*. Tonight, he's mine. Thank you."

Meanwhile Phil finds out that one of our pro-MMA fighters has been training the kid. And at seven o'clock after work I'm at Phil's ready for this kid. Phil has really not seen me enraged quite like this. He says, "You sure he's going to show?"

I reply, "Oh yeah. He'll be here." Just then Lee and Luke walk in, saying '*hello*', they go to the back part of Phil's basement gym to warm up. They're going to work ground. No one else is in yet.

Just after seven o'clock the kid pulls up. I say to Phil, "He's here. I told yah."

The kid comes in, he gets settled. Then Phil says to him, "Jody, says you've got talent. Once you warm-up, she will do three five minute professional MMA rounds with you. Okay?"

The kid says, "Yeah."

The kid comes in, I smile as we shake hands. And before we know it, we're going at it. He lands a kick to the crotch. I ignore it. But Phil sees it, stops him and says, "That's illegal. You can't do that." Phil looks at me. I keep a straight face. He's wondering if I feel it. I know I'm fracture there, but I've been through worse. I'll suck it up.

Then Antonio comes in and says 'hi'. We resume, still in the first round. As Antonio stretches, Luke and Lee pause their wrestling. I see them watching us out of the corner of my eye.

Antonio slouches on the ground just outside the roped off cage where this kid and I fight. Phil is the referee. The kid does another combination with kick to the crotch again. Again like Friday night, I grab him and put him into a guillotine and this time, I elbow his ribs, he's tapping. Phil says nothing. Antonio yells, "Phil the kids' tapping."

Phil says, "Oh I didn't see it." We restart. Then the first round bell goes off. I have him in a guillotine again and punching and elbowing the kid.

Antonio says, "Jody, the bell went off."

Phil says, "Yes, that's the end of the first round."

I respond like I'm stupid, "*Ohhh* Okay." I play stupid
very well. All those years in corporate, when you call
someone a '*lazy son of a bitch*', but you didn't say that.
You said it more tactfully. I wasn't called *The Charmer*
by a boss for nothing. And the person you aimed it at
tilted their head, wondered and you just smiled back at
them like you're stupid.
   The second round bell goes off. We begin. As we
spar I grab, and release just as he's ready to tap. I do this
with an elbow or a few punches to the ribs holding him
in guillotine and then, as he is ready to tap I release.
Before the end of the second round, he's had enough.
Phil calls it.
   I look to my left, Antonio is looking at me with a
queried look. And the look Luke and Lee gave me was
one of wonderment. Later after Lee, Luke and the kid
leave at end of session. Antonio hears what was going
on. He says, "Oh man, I was wondering."

Phil says, "You were so enraged. You were almost
losing it."

I responded, "Yep. That couldn't have come faster. I
had a really painful weekend. I'm still bleeding to my
left knee." Antonio saw it. Lifted up my board short
pant leg about five inches from the knee and there was
the skin discolored deep purple from the bleeding from

the pubic bone area. "Running has been tough the last few days too. I think I'll be able to sleep tonight."

Phil asks, "You feel better?"

I reply, "Mentally. Yes, I had to get that out of my system. And I like to take care of my own business."

Well as the days came and went. Friday night again was upon us. This time Antonio and Bruno and a bunch of others were in. The kid was in. Unknown to me, Bruno heard about what the kid did and he was pissed.

Antonio and Bruno asked the kid if they could spar with him. The kid feeling like they would go easy on him, no one said anything. He said, "Sure."

So first Antonio went with him, the kid could take it a little, then he seemed to quit on Antonio. The kid was dismayed. Antonio asked, "What? You *quitin'*?"

The kid responded, "No…"

Then Bruno said, "Hey, I'll spar with you." The kid agreed. I was in the back corner of the gym working in the boxing ring with someone. Before I know it, the kid is crying and Bruno says, "You can't take it? You don't think it's fair."

Then one of the guys says, "Hey, Bruno. Stop. The kids crying, man."

Bruno stops and says, "Now you sit down here." He has the kid sit on a heavy bag on the gym floor. Bruno continues, "You see that woman over there in the ring? That's my mother! Well, like my mother! She's my gym mother. Now you go and apologize to her."

Now the kid is really crying, I hear him sobbing as he approaches the ring and I'm working with someone. He then apologizes. I thank him. Funny, the guys hurt the kid's pride, and not the kid.

In the end he ended up being not such a punk. And Phil found out who trained him and some words exchanged.

The guy that trained him, also corrected the kid. I felt he was this misguided kid, who thought taking down someone in Phil's basement gym would make him a 'big' man. Instead it got him in trouble. Now he leads a very successful life. He changed, and his life got better.

Life's Struggles

Everyday when she awakes,
No one knows what mind goes through.
No matter what she makes,
Many misconstrue.

The existence of her bewilders some.
And many cannot cope,
 Their miseries they put on her,
 Would douse most people's hope.

She struggles every morning,
Finding some semblance of reason.
No matter how she smiles,
Darts fly through every season.

The day she understood this,
Her life became more pleasing.
And now progressing forward,
She only does what is appeasing.

Figure 11. Danbury Connecticut 2012 Cornered Ray in white shirt. Toby wanted to watch men fight.

Chapter Thirty
I'm not here to sing Kumbaya (2013)

Probably one of the most wicked years of my life in athletics, was 2013. I had five fights between February 23rd, 2013 and June 8th 2013. That was year I went pro in MMA. That was the first full year Phil had his new big gym, *Asylum Fight Gym*. It was huge. That year going into the next would test Phil, myself, and many others.

On Friday December 21st 2012, Phil calls me as I'm entering the gym. I answer, "Yeah Phil. What's up?"

He's frustrated, "I was driven off the road, on my way down. Mike is going to train you. I need to get towed, I'm in a ditch on the side of the *Saw Mill Parkway*."

I respond, "Are you okay?"

Phil replies, "Yeah, I'm just pissed. I've now waited about thirty minutes or so to get towed. I don't even know the damage. The guy ran into my lane and I went to avoid him."

I replied, "Okay, no problem. Mike cool with it?"

Phil responds, "Yes, I told him. He said he'd train with you."

I replied, "Okay good. Alright, just be safe."

Afterwards, Mike and I talk as I get ready. Mike is working my form and helping train me. Then Mike says, "You want to spar a little?"

I respond, "Oh yeah. That'd be great." We hadn't sparred together in a long while. He has a different style, and he's not as tall as Phil. So it would give me a different look in sparring.

We go at it. Finally, I'm throwing the cross the way Mike had drilled it with me. Landing the cross so well, that I had nailed him a number of times. And landed right in the solar plexus that he said, "Hold on. I got to breath."

I asked, "Is that okay?"

Mike replied, "Yeah it was good." We begin again. I land again. He had to stop for a few seconds catch his breath. Then we would go again. I landed five times that stopped him out of ten attempts.
I could feel the power, but I really didn't know any other aspect to the punch I was throwing. Phil had always said, "You get that punch off right, you're going to do some damage."

Soon the sparring and training session was over. I thanked Mike and paid him. Mike said, "Those were really good shots Jody."

I responded, "Thanks. I hope Phil is okay."

Then he went to do some phone calling and I went to get changed. People were funneling through, as Vlad was about to arrive and teach the Sambo Class.

I was in the locker room and as I unwrapped my left-hand, I saw something was wrong on the dorsal side (top) of the hand behind the ring finger and its knuckle by about an inch and a half. I thought to myself, '*Oh God no. Not another infection*'. I had just had a long bout of an infection in my right shin back in the third week of October and it wouldn't go away. I missed training, then had to go light for a while on antibiotics for fourteen days. They didn't know what I had.

That all started when I fractured my right foot on Killer Ken doing a demonstration of how I should maneuver in a *takedown* defense. That had happened on Thursday, October 18th 2012. Phil had to cancel two of my November fights because of that. The last time a fight had to be canceled for me was October 1st 2011, when I had another injury.

I was able to run painfully with the fracture in my foot, but could not get kicked or work takedowns for a bit then I got the infection days later, I was in screaming hot pain in my right shin, just laying down and I had a fever. I felt pretty ill. We didn't know what it was. There was no cut. We thought cellulitis.

Phil spoke with my doctor's colleague on Monday October 22nd, at night before class. I came and showed Phil my leg. And he was concerned, so I called my internist's office immediately and the doctor said, "Is your fight trainer with you now? "

I responded, "Yes. You want to speak with him?"

The doctor said, "Yes." I handed Phil the phone.

They chatted briefly of what Phil thought it was. The doctor then said, "I'll call in an antibiotic, tell me the pharmacy you use and what can you take? I want you to call the office tomorrow and see your doctor this week."

I replied, "Okay, will do."

Now here it was a six weeks past finishing the antibiotic and I made certain I hadn't sparred too soon, to protect my musculoskeletal system. Now here I was looking at it, hoping it wasn't another infection for I had a fight schedule in the Bronx on January 26th 2013. I wanted the fight badly.

So Ryan comes into the locker room. I say, "Yo, Ryan."

Ryan responds, "Yes."

I show him my hand and ask, "What's this?"

Ryan replied, "Oh. You broke your hand."

I reply, "Thank God!"

Ryan looks at me with a head tilt and a weird look.

I continue, "Hey, don't tell anybody. I'll suck it up. I'm just glad it's not another infection. *Shhhhh.* No one needs to know."

Ryan says, "No problem."

I reply, "I got to make that fight in five weeks, man."

Then I get dressed, and just as I'm ready to go. Phil calls me on my cell, "Jody I'm so sorry. How did it go with Mike?"

I replied, "Oh great. It was a great training session. Thanks. I got to spar too. I think I'm getting sharper quicker."

Phil responds, "Oh good. What a *shitty* day. I just got my car towed and I am now at a shop to see what the damage is. Can you ask Vlad, if he can close up?"

I reply, "Yeah, sure."

Phil responded, "Thank you. I will be there tomorrow morning, even if I have to borrow a car."

Then we say '*good-bye*' and I get off the phone and relay the message to Mike and Vlad. Vlad is cool with it.

The next morning, Saturday, December 22nd 2012, I come in at nine forty in the morning. My left hand, is not terrible, just buzzing and a little achy feeling. I took arnica pellets, iced and used my arnica rescue concoction the night before and that morning. I figure Phil won't want to spar today with me.

I drop my stuff into the locker room entrance and call to Phil. He responds, "Yes."

I walk in and ask, "How you *doin'*?

Phil replies, "Uh alright. Better than yesterday. Jody I was so beside myself."

I ask, "So you good now?"

Phil replies, "Uh, real good."

I say, "I had a great session with Mike yesterday we sparred. I landed well. It stopped him. However, uh very minor thing."

Phil responded, "What's that?"

I reply, "Well, I'll be fine for January 26th fight. And I want it bad. Uh. I kind of sort of broke my left hand on Mike last night before you called."

Phil responds, "Oh. I'm so glad you didn't tell me that last night."

I reply, "I thought so. But don't pull me, I'm fine. I got this."

Phil responded, "We will see how you feel."

I reply, "Yeah but I'm fine. I'm sure."

Phil says, "I'm going to spar with you today."

I reply, "Uh. Okay." Before we know it the place is getting filled the kickboxing people are in with their instructor. I'm working ground, then stand up drills and some '*live*' work with some of the guys. My hand I wrapped is not so bad inside my four ounce glove.
Then Phil asks, "You warmed up?"

I reply, "Yeah."

Phil gets gloves and shin pads on. Phil waves me into the small training cage we have in the new gym. Then he says, "Let's *move*."
And so we do. I don't feel my left hand at all. I make it through the thirty minute sparring session with Phil, While Peter and Tom roll outside our area on the expansive wrestling area. Every once in a while someone comes by to watch or the guys rolling stop, come by and watch.
Then it was time for me to get cleaned up, go and do family stuff, to have family time as well. My left hand didn't feel so bad. I had cooking and baking to do for Christmas. That would end up being the test for my left hand.
By Sunday, December 23rd, my left hand was having a tough time holding a yam to peel. But I figured, '*it would be okay Monday for practice*'. Plus not a lot of bodies to work on, due the fact it was Christmas Eve. I kept it light so I could prep, cook, make pies, and other food stuff for Christmas Day.

Soon Monday came we had practice for lunch, and Phil said, "You ready?"

I replied, "Yeah, well. I'm a little more pained than Saturday, but I really didn't feel anything as we sparred then."

Phil replied, "We will work your cage entrance. 'Cause I worked you good on Saturday. This will give you recovery into Wednesday night, because of the holiday."

I responded, "Okay."

Mike and Jack were over on the other side of the red matted wrestling area and we were just fifteen feet from the boxing ring. It was very quiet due to the fact that it was Christmas Eve.

So the first attempted attack I missed. The second attack attempted I felt some pain in throwing the combination.

Phil said, "We will see how you do. I don't want to push it."

I said, "Okay. I got cooking to do, and only a few bodies after this. I should be okay."

Then the third attack attempt I made. The pain hit. The pain in my hand shot through me. I yelped, and hit the deck. "Sorry Phil. I didn't expect that. Let me try again."

Phil said, "I think you should do ground or we should work kicks. Give the hand a rest."

I saw Mike look over at me and say, "What happened?"

Phil says, "She broke her hand."

So after we decided to have me do ground, before I knew it session was over, I was cleaned up and going to work. That night the left hand was so bad our daughters had to help me peel apples and potatoes. I didn't try and commandeer them till I couldn't handle anymore pain, and could no longer grip with the left hand.

As the holiday passed, I worked on drilling to throw correctly and my ground game. I also worked increasing fresh pineapple, my green vegetables, and I was vigorous in self-therapy to get my left hand to heal better.

Soon, seventeen days later I was able to punch full force with a twelve ounce glove on with my left hand wrapped. At the same time, the first opponent for the fight had a snowboarding accident and was in surgery.

We had another opponent and as I was totally healed within ten days of the fight, Phil and I knew I was ready. The new opponent all of a sudden we realized she'd not been posting or chatting about this fight. About three days before the fight the coach announced that she had pulled out. This was with no reason given.

By this time, we had about eighty-six people pull out of I don't know how many fight offers. Either the coach pulled them, they pulled, or something else we couldn't figure.

As Phil would say, "That's the fight business and you're in a tough weight-class. These girl's don't really want to fight a woman twice their age. They think at first it would be an easy fight. Then on second thought, someone talks into their ear and then they realize upon watching your tapes that you strike. And if they win, they beat an old person. If they lose they look real bad."

I'd shrug, not really understanding certain mentality, yet work on accepting it. It was the very thing we knew we may be up against, prejudices.
Then the next fight I was offered was February 23rd 2013, an exhibition for a 128 pound boxer ready to retire. We got the call on Monday, February 18th 2013. Phil called me from Sambo Wrestling practice with Vlad. I entered Phil's office.

Phil asked, "How would you like an exhibition boxing match?"

I answered without hesitation, "I'll take it."

Phil responded, "You don't even know how much she weighs."

I replied, "I don't care. It's boxing man I'll take it. But one problem. Do I got to wear those boxing shoes? 'Cause I can't get them just now. I have no time this week."

Phil responded, "I'll make it work. It's an exhibition. The girl sold tickets and John wants to make this happen for her, 'cause she's retiring. But you got to wear head gear."

I replied, "Okay. I never did that before. But I do have head gear. *Ummm*, I'll go for a few runs with it on this week. Let me know."

Phil said, "Okay, good. I'll work the foot gear issue out."

I respond, "Oh great. Thanks."

Just about twenty minutes later, I guess I caught a chill, my right sacroiliac joint goes out and the pain is coming from my right hip graphing surgical site I had from April 13th, 1993. I walk into Phil's office hunched. "Uh, Phil fix me. I'll show you how?"

Phil asks, "What's wrong?"

I reply, "My right sacroiliac (S.I. joint) is out. My graphing site just flared up." I lay down and instruct Phil how to get the joint back to where it should be and get me out of pain and spasm. It worked. I get up, "Okay, I'm fine."

Every day and every session Phil had to fix my S.I. joint area. The pain continued. I told Phil, "I'm running with the head gear five to ten miles a day. I should be adjusted to it by Thursday. That will give me three days of running with it on."

Phil shakes his head, "No you couldn't two or three miles. It's got to be a marathon."

Soon Saturday approaches and I realize something, but I don't tell Phil. The day is cloudy, damp and raw. A condition I've had most of my life flares up, Raynaud's. Effecting a few of my fingers and my right distal foot area. I blast the heat in my minivan.

It takes me about ninety minutes to drive up to the event site. I'm in S.I. joint pain the whole way. The only thing that seems to help this is resting my graphing site on a tennis ball as I drive. Driving in this condition with my right S.I. joint in spasm is the pits, and painful as anything.

I get up there, then we weigh me in with most my clothing on and I'm 108 pounds. She weighs in around 128 pounds and I don't see her, she went to eat. I asked Phil, "Hey can you check my leg-length. I think it's a little off. I'm feeling a little rigid from pain, so loosened me up and I'll be fine. I'm good."

Phil looks at me, "You look drawn. Are you sure?"

I respond, "Phil I need this." What Phil didn't know and I completely had put out of my mind all month was this day was the anniversary of my brother's death seven years before. It didn't dawn on me till after the event was over.

Phil kept checking in with me. He was uncertain about my body. He said, "Maybe I should pull you. Jody, you don't look right."

I replied, "Phil, I need this please. I really need this so bad. Please."

Phil responded, "Okay. Okay."

I responded, "I'm okay. I'll make it good. Once I get in there I'll be fine."

Soon enough, we are called to the ring, I have no shoes. She has boxing shoes on. Otherwise everything else is equal. I'm scared, jittery. Yet, I know I need this in my life right now. She looks real tough and has a thick build. And with a nickname like '*Danger*', I take it seriously.

The start of the first round is on. I'm super jittery, in the first minute of the first round, she seems to have an advantage. Then towards the end I realize I can do this. Then the second round we go at it again. I'm having fun. I'm cornering her. I can't believe I'm cornering a boxer lady. I never thought I would have any skills like this or be able to apply them.

Then the second round ends and Phil and Mark say, "Jody, you're doing good. Put pressure on her just like you did in the second round."

I reply, "Okay. I think I feel good."

Figure 12. February 23rd, 2013, Rachel 'Danger' Campbell, and I.

Then the third round starts and I go at it aggressively like Phil had told me to. Again, I now have the advantage. I can see my stamina kicking in. However, the only problem is I cannot feel the right foot at all. And the left foot is numb at the bottom of the foot.

My Raynaud's has kicked in massively. I have no clue how I'm going to stand on my feet, without feeling what's underneath them. Somehow I manage and the third round ends. The boxing lady Rachel hugs me. I think to myself. *'I may have done something good'*.

Phil and Mark, are pleasantly surprised and so is her coach. I gave her a good go of it. And that was my job, besides getting in some good free sparing. As we shake hands and hug again. I'm having a tough time getting out of the ring. I held someone's shoulder to not fall, because I couldn't feel my feet. My right foot was completely numb. I looked down at the right foot it is jet red on top and the toes which are so pained are pure white. It's as though I just plastered a piece of white printer paper on them to cover them up.

As Phil, Mark and Lorraine are standing by me on the gymnasium floor. I ask, "How'd I do?"

Phil replied, "Jody, you did great.... How do you feel?"

I replied almost laughing, "Well my back and S.I. joint no longer hurting. *Buuuut*, see my feet? They are numb on the bottoms and my right foot hurts really badly at the toes. My Raynaud's Syndrome flared up a bit today. Look down at them."

269

They looked down at my feet. I continue, "I need to put my shoes on now. I'm getting really cold. I can't feel anything."

Mark turned to me and said, "You really did well. I did not expect that."

I asked, "Really?"
Mark repeated himself and then said, "Really. She is a boxer. She has experience. When did you take this fight?"

I replied, "Uh, Monday."

Seated now, awaiting to watch the rest of the fights. Mark said, "Well it's hard to get you fights. You could always fight in Burma."

I look over Mark's back and say to Phil, "Mark says I'd get more fights in my weight-class in Burma. What do yah say, Phil?"

Phil answers, "Mark's correct. You never know."

Mark says, "Well I wasn't saying you should go. I'm just saying you'd get more fights your size."

Phil says, "Well, it's an idea."

The next week Phil says, "There's MMA fight in New York. They want to have you be part of the main event."

I reply, "I'll take it."

Phil responds, "The girl is bigger than you. Got good *takedowns*. I'll let them know."

We chat about it and how Phil is going to train me to try something new. What he realizes but not at that moment is, I'm having a tough time learning athletically certain movements, especially level changes. I've been that way all my life, it took me till I was eight years old to ride a bike. This is due to birth defects and lack of being able to balance.

In the end we accept the fight. The fight becomes a debacle of sorts. The venue is changed three times and the third time it is moved after weigh-ins and about twenty-four hours before the event is to take place.

They scramble to find a new event location and it is settled by about eight at night the night before the event takes place. Then the day of the fight, many pull out. Then more fighters and coaches are pulling out, when they found out that the cage is delivered without the proper equipment. Mats are brought in from a variety of sizes, not fitting the cage construction. There are lumps in the flooring. Then the referee doesn't show up. Then there is no real medical staff backup.

I now have some trepidation as others do, but I don't want to throwaway an opportunity to fight. I fear disappointing Phil. All our fighters take the fights. Many fighters bail where they had a full fight card. Now the fight card is six or seven fights as opposed to about fourteen fights.

The guy who steps up as a referee had minimal experience and never refereed a woman's fight. He finds out I'm fifty years of age. He sees me mess up defending a *takedown*, my opponent is hitting my body and it's not phasing me. I'm calm, because I've been in this position before and it was by far much worse.

I'm relaxed, then I hear Phil, "Ref, she's okay! She's okay!"

Then the ref stops the fight. I'm like what's going on. I ask, "What??!"

The guy who was refereeing says, "You're fifty. You should be happy you got in the cage."

Trying not to be disrespectful, I say, "What??! You're kidding me. I have no damage. I was calm. Getting hit is not a problem! You're kidding me?!" I am so upset.

I lose because the guy is not a referee and he panics because he finds out my age, but knows nothing about me. I am devastated. I figure, *'no one will ever let me fight again.'*

I leave the cage with Phil, back stage I lose it. I don't know what to think. I figure, *'Phil will never have confidence in me fighting ever again.'* Phil is trying to keep me from losing it. But I just can't help it. I felt set up. I now didn't know who I could trust. Phil does everything to convince me that it wasn't about me. It was a debacle. It's just a wicked night. And probably one of the worst times in any athletics I'd ever experienced.

I don't remember driving home. I was so distraught.

Not Exactly Don Juan...and The Liberated Woman

The next day, I go for a run, then I in between work and family of a Monday I go to Phil's *Asylum Fight Gym* to train. Somewhere that night training, Phil has spoken with me to see where my head is at. Then he receives a phone call from a matchmaker. They have a 115 pound girl, Viktoria Makarova. It's another promotion that Phil had a couple guys that were to fight from our team on the card. One guy couldn't, he had a lung infection. The other guy was on the card. He was a real up and comer.

Phil asks, "It's this Saturday. You want it?"

I reply, "Yeah! I'll take it. Where is it?"

Phil responds, "It's in Manhattan at the Hammerstein Ballroom. It's big Jody. It's to decide who represents the U.S. to go to Korea to compete in MMA as an amateur."

I reply, "I wouldn't turn that down for the world. Put me in. I'll tell Norman. It'll be good."

Phil responded, "Okay, you got to be within three pounds of her and she's very tall."

I reply, "I can do it. I know I weigh about 105 right now. When is weigh-ins?"

Phil responds, "Friday afternoon. The fights are Saturday night."

I replied, "Okay. Lots of water. I'll cut back on my running a little. I'll eat carbs. I'll drink water. I think I can drink about seven pounds of water right before the weigh-ins. What do you want me to weigh?"

Phil responds, "Try to weigh about 112 or so."

I replied, "Okay. So you do still believe in me Phil?"

Phil responded, "Jody, its okay. Let's move forward. These people want you. You deserve this opportunity."

I replied, "Thank you Phil."

Friday, March 22nd 2013 soon arrived. It had been just six days before when I thought I would never compete again. Talk about a 180 degree turn around of emotions. This was huge. The promotion, *Fight Source* had a good plan and wanted to start implementing it.

The weigh-ins were in a hotel conference room, where the fighter and their coach/trainer had to register. Then weigh in. Ethan and I were there to weigh-in for our fights. Phil drove us together from the *Asylum Fight Gym* parking lot. I sat and spoke with Ethan as Phil drove us.

I double checked to see how much I had to weigh. Once again, I realized I was staying at 105. So I began to drink water as time got closer to weigh-in. I knew from my running ultra-races that twenty ounces of water was approximately two point three pounds of weight.

Finally after calculating that I needed almost three twenty-four ounce sport bottles of water ingested just before I weighed-in. I would see if they let me wear my shirt, undershirt, bra, and pants. Then I would have to drink only sixty ounces of water. So that would be two and a half twenty-four ounce sport bottles of water, approximately. Or three twenty ounce bottles of water.

Then within twenty-five minutes of me filling up, they called my name to weigh-in. I was dying. I thought I was going to urinate in my pants. I weigh-in 112.9 pounds. Viktoria Makarova, who seemed quite tall near five foot eight inches tall, wore the smallest bikini I think I'd ever seen. She weighed-in at 113.6, from what I can recall. It was a *go*. But I couldn't leave to go to the bathroom. I had to stand and pose with her for pictures. I was in some mighty discomfort.

Finally, they let me go and I ran to the ladies room. I didn't think I'd make it. There were two open stalls. *'Thank God!'* I thought to myself. I must've urinated for about five minutes. It was quite amazing. I thought, *'I should've timed it. I probably would've set a record for the longest pee.'*

Then after I got back to the conference room, Phil, Ethan and I were ready to get going back home. Ethan was hungry. I was well-hydrated.

The next afternoon, I would be on my own driving into the city for the event. I left early. And I arrived at the Parking Garage near the Hammerstein Ballroom. Then I went inside. I ducked away up into the balcony area hallways, till Phil and Ethan got there. Then we had blood pressure checks, fight rules, and then shown where the back stage set-ups were for each corner.

I tried silent meditation however, it wasn't going to happen. I was super-nervous. I actually couldn't remember my walk out song. I just was so much more interested in the fight itself. Many of our teammates came to watch. The place was packed before we knew it. And this was first time that they didn't let the fight trainers wrap their own fighter's hands. I didn't like it. But they insisted we comply. So we did.

After Ethan and I were wrapped, they did the usual double checks on the wrapping of the fighter's hands and sign off on them. Ethan was soon up and he fought a kid from the Midwest. The kid was very experienced. He threw a head kick at Ethan and it lacerated his face in the first round so badly, the referee stopped the fight. Ethan was so devastated.

When I awaited my fight, I was so cold, even after I warmed up. I hoped the cage area was warmer. There were bunch of us to walk me down. It was, Eric, Mike, Kyle, Ray, and Phil. You only could have a couple guys in your corner for coaching during the event, but the walk down was okay.

They played some weird music that I had not chosen. It was way not me. It was way too girly and whiney sounding. They announced my name, "Viktoria Makarova." I had to keep from laughing. I really didn't care.

Then I was hugged by my teammates, checked, and was escorted into the cage. Then my music played and Viktoria Makarova walked out to my music and into the cage. They reviewed the rules, set the timers, checked with the officials and it was a *go*.

I came out fast and aggressive. She was stunned. However, I made the mistake of pausing after chasing her down and she managed at some point in the first round to get a *takedown*. She attempted to do damage, but to no avail.

The bell sounded the end of the first round. I was so elated, no one freaked out and tried to stop it like just six nights before. It was a major emotional hurdle for me to keep my calm and not think this referee too would know my age and freak out. So as I walked back to my corner, where Phil was waiting for me, I started to giggle.

Phil has this dumbfounded look on his face and asks, "Are you okay?" I'm giggling, trying not to snort laugh. I felt high actually. The referee seeing this appeared quite humored. He probably never saw a woman get mounted in a cage fight, punched in the face and such, and take it lightly. But that wasn't the point. It was that I was being given a fair chance to fight. Phil sat me down, checked me out, and sip of water I refused. Phil, told me to try and stop laughing. I smiled as I focused on my opponent across the cage.

I stood up so fast and was jumping up and down while she was still seated. Then the sound came that it was end of the one minute rest and the second round was to begin in seconds.

She stood, the referee checked to see if everyone was ready and the second round began. I launched the same attack. And she threw a nice kick to the inside of my right knee. I attempted to trade with her, but it appeared she wanted no real trading on the feet. Soon she got another *takedown*. This time she seemed more determined than before. I wanted to exhaust her on the ground. So I grabbed onto her body from beneath her like a baby koala bear. She was using much energy and I figured at some point she won't be able to even submit

277

me, let alone punch me, and somehow she could make a mistake. Then I figured, I could get some advantage and make it the game changer in my favor.

Soon again the second round ended. Now she was getting tired. I actually saw my energy on the tele-tron at one point behind her above. I saw me jumping up and down and her slouching on the stool in her corner. I thought, *'I may have her. She doesn't have my stamina. And she doesn't like getting punched neither'*.

Shortly after those thoughts the third round began. Again I attacked and seemingly kept it on the feet a bit longer. I was now warmed up. Even still she got another *takedown*. However, this one wasn't as effective as the other two *takedowns*. She was weakened. I could feel it. I got her in my guard and she had nowhere to go. I went for a guillotine. I heard my corner people and teammates yelling. Just when I thought I'd have it. I made a mistake and she smartly capitalized on it. I forgot to pin her down with my right leg when holding the guillotine with my left arm. She eventually eased over my right leg and got half mount.

There was a point before this I remember her getting so frustrated with me, she head butted my face. And Phil screamed, "Ref! That was a head butt!"

I ignored it as if it never happened. I'd been beat up by Phil and the guys so much nothing after that ever mattered from a woman.

Soon enough the third round was over. I knew she won on points. It would come down to a decision. But I knew she was the better fighter that night. We got up and she walked over to her coach nearly crying. I went over to console her. I grabbed her arm. Held it in the air and said, "You won. You hear me. Kudos to you. You did great!" As I raised her arm and pointed to her that she won. I let the audience know, that I made no bones about it.

Soon Phil came into the cage we shook hands with her trainer, others and then the referee brought us to the center and her hand was raised. She had won the decision as I knew so. We hugged and then departed. She got interviewed by Bruce Kivo. Bruce Kivo was of the *Underground* interviewed her. Then Bruce interviewed me after all the fights were over as well.

Figure 13. Hammerstein Ballroom 2013 The Walk-out

Chapter Thirty-One
CRAAZEEE! (2013)

After the fights ended at the Hammerstein Ballroom, I was cleaning up, taking my time and Phil and a bunch of the guys left as the promoter's crew were cleaning up. Feeling relaxed, I chatted with two of the security guards. I knew I would take my time leaving I was too awake to go to sleep anytime soon.

And then I saw one of our guys. I found out he was stranded. His friends whom Phil and I didn't really like, left him high and dry with no ride back to his home somewhere near the Connecticut border. I text my husband and said, 'I'm fine. One of the guys needs a ride. He needs help. I'll be home by four (in the morning).'

I commandeered the young man. I was old enough to be his mother and asked, "Hey, yo! Where's your drive?

He answered, "Where's Phil?"

I answered, "He left. Who'd you come with?"

He responded, "They left. We had an argument."

I said, "I'll take you home. You tell me where you live. I'll drive you home."

He responded, "Really?"

I replied, "Yes, *Com'on*. My minivan is around the corner. *Com'on*. I'll drive you home."

He was upset. We walked to the parking garage where my minivan was. I paid the attendant, and tipped him. The young man was still feeling bad.

I said, "Hey, don't worry. I got you."

He said, "I feel so bad. I did one thing wrong and they bailed on me."

We got into my minivan. I continued, "You know you can talk to me. So what happened to your two friends?"

He said, "Jody you saved me. They told me I was a fool. Right when you called my name I was going to meet those guys from the Midwest at a bar. I was going to go drinking with them. I was all set. Then you called my name. I felt lost. I didn't know where Phil was. I was depressed. I can't believe they left me."

I did know this young man had a number of problems. But he was one of these what I call, *'suffering alive'* people. I knew this well. I'd seen in my lifetime, throughout my childhood, and into my adult years. And if they were kind and nice in a general way, I would wonder to myself, *'God, why do tender-souls who are nice people have to have such diseases? What does this prove, anyway?'*

I asked, "What'd you do wrong? You can tell me."

282

He answered, "I had a beer. I'm not allowed to drink. They got on my case."

I replied, "So you made a mistake. It's okay. We are human and tomorrow is another day. A *do-over*, if you will. And besides, you didn't go drinking with those guys from the Midwest. You're smart. Give yourself credit."

As the young man unloaded on how it all transpired and how their friendship had originally came to be years ago. The young man said, "I can't believe I'm telling you all this. I'm so sorry."

I replied, "It's quite alright. You're human. Everybody goes through rough times. It's really okay. I couldn't slept tonight anyway. Also, you came out and supported me. You're a great team-mate. Thank you."

We chatted for about ninety minutes as I drove him home. I said, "You know. You want to hear what I think of that one guy?"

He said, "Huh?"

I replied, "He's a jackass. Good for nothin'. Got no balls. And he's a girl. You got me. He'd rat on his own mother, just to get ahead. You see what I'm saying?"

He laughed and said, "Wow! That's what you see?"

I replied, "Yep. He's no man. I saw it on January 26th in your fight. The young man thinks he knows everything. He's a jerk, and he's not your friend. You know. Phil knows that. Phil cares about you, you know. He really does."

Soon enough we got to the guys home, and he had a tough time getting in, not setting off the security code. I told him when you get settled, you text me in about an hour. Let me know you're cool. Okay?"

He replied, "Yeah. Thank you Jody. I can't believe you listened to me."

I answered, "Anytime. You got it. You're a good guy."

He texted me as I asked by the time I got home. I called him. I heard his voice and we said, *'goodnight'*.

The next morning I let Phil know to check up on him, Phil did. He thanked me. Phil lived up near the kid. They had a good talk.

Figure 14. Hammerstein Ballroom March 23rd, 2013.

Chapter Thirty-Two
Two main events...When it rains it Pours(2013)

A couple days later I was back in the gym training. I felt renewed. Then Phil says, "Fight Source wants you to fight a girl at 105 for a title fight, and for another shot at making the USA team for the amateur fight in Korea. You want it?"

I reply, "I'll take it." I'm psyched as usual. The fight is in five weeks in Dania Beach, Florida.

Phil says, "She's got good, ground and she's got judo. Your striking is better. I'm going to send you a video of her to watch."

I replied, "Okay."

During that time Phil is keeping me on my toes and he spars me once a week. I'm also sparring some of the other guys throughout the week. Our sparring sessions with others on stand-up are anywhere from fifteen to forty minutes a day.

Usually, Phil will have more than one guy willing to spar with me. I tire them out. Some are done in the ring, some of the stand-up is done in the cage. As our usual tradition we don't wear headgear. So it makes you be less stupid.

However, within two weeks of the fight, I get a couple injuries. Phil knows something isn't right, but I am able to ignore it. Ten days out my right hand doesn't feel so good. When you spar with four ounce gloves on and you're hitting brick walls that are bigger than you. Sometimes things fracture.

However, at this point I don't care. I want that title, we are the co-main event. It is the third or fourth time I'm in either the main event or co-main event, in my fight career.

Then by the time we have ten days to go to the event, Phil says, "I got some good news and some bad news. Katie Couture, you know Randy Couture's wife? She's a matchmaker for this fight out in Colorado. It's a pro fight. The girl is ranked about four or five in the world. She's nine and six. She's a beast. Katie told me they went through like seven or eight fighters. No one wanted to fight her."

I respond, "I'll take it."

Phil remarks, "Wait, so you would go for this title fight, and what if you made the U.S. A. Team?"

I replied, "I'll take it. Hey, I don't know how long I can do this. Or how long anyone will let me do this. What do you think?"

Phil says, "It's up to you."

I respond, "I think this is a golden opportunity. I mean *hec*. Why not? I'm so amazed I got this opportunity. Let's do it."

Phil replied, "Okay, I'll call them and tell them. Plus all your medicals are up to date. They do the pregnancy test there."

I responded, "Okay, good."

As we prepare for this Monday night title fight in Dania Beach, Florida on April 22nd, 2013, perhaps making the U.S.A. MMA team to go to Korea. We get other offers. We now have to turn them down, which is not something we had to do before.

Soon enough it is time to travel to Florida. The weigh-ins are Sunday evening April 21st, 2013. We are picked up by one of the promoter's assistants, and brought to the event's weigh-in registration area.

I have all my paperwork. I weigh-in at the correct weight of 105. My opponent was 108. The Athletic Commissioner has this look in his eye, he finds out that I am fifty years of age. He declares the EKG that I've had done recently needs to be redone. He wants me to go to a local fire house to have it done. They're screwing with me. I don't really get it.

Phil said, "It's not about you."

I responded quietly to Phil, 'What the *hec*? I'm tired. They are trying tire me more. I got to eat and rest." Everyone had the paperwork so it seemed but the athletic commissioner. Ridiculous. It was a head-shaker but I remained calm.

The promoter said, "Here's the fight doctor's number. Use him to get any additional medicals the commissioner wants Jody to get." He hands the information to Phil.

Phil decides that night to rent a car after we get a taxi from the weigh-ins to the hotel. After we check in, he is able to rent a car. Then we get out to eat. Our normal chat routine while I gorge myself with steak and Phil woofs down six baked potatoes, begins. Now that we've traveled all over together since January 7th 2011, Phil is used to the waitress' look when I order thirty ounces of steak for the meal the night before the fight.

We discuss fight plans and Phil lets me know how he sees the fight. It is overcast. The weather is to be rainy both days we are there. The next morning I get up drink some barley grass, water and coffee, call Norman and then go for a run. My last call home before I shut down my mind completely before the fight takes place.

I find a coffee shop while out running four miles. I come back and buzz Phil and let him know about it. He tells me we have an appointment at the fight doctor's clinic at about eleven that morning.

Soon we arrive at the clinic. I fill out the necessary paperwork. They check me and set up the EKG. Also the doctor does other precautionary tests, like another pregnancy test. He, the doctor and his staff are very professional and he knows that all this is a political move of some kind.

He gets done with my EKG and reads it. At first he wonders why it looks so different from most peoples. Then Phil says, "Here's the one she had a month ago."

They are the same. Then Phil told him of my crazy running.

Then the doctor comparing the two EKGs responds, "Oh, she's a real athlete. That makes a lot of sense."

Phil said, "Yeah."

I reply, "You know, most people wouldn't understand my lows and highs. But my resting pulse is forty-two to forty-five upon waking, and fifty-two between three and seven at night, after a full day of work and training."

The three of us chat for about another twenty minutes. The doctor says, "You're good. Here's a copy of the EKG, and I'll bring the hard copy, so no one has a problem."

Soon as we are about to enter fight venue, the dark storm clouds are encroaching. You can smell the heavy rain air, as the fighters and the trainers are awaiting the doors to open and have the rules meeting.

We get in as the storm is coming in. Rules meeting, the athletic commissioner is still saying he never received the fight doctor's report or any blood work. However, the promoter, the matchmaker, and Phil have it all on their phones. So do I. The athletic commissioner is saying he can't see it. I'm staying calm. I know that someone wants to either stop this fight or frustrate us so we get tired. *It's real bullshit*, I think.

The athletic commissioner was sent my results of the day from the fight doctor as well. Finally the fight doctor gets there and shows the athletic commissioner all the paperwork, the hard copies. They call me up to the table in the event area, as a torrential downpour continues. There is a leak through the tent like tarp they put up and it's dripping on electrical equipment that the fighters have to step over on their way to the cage, right before they fight.

Upon receiving the hard copies of paperwork, the doctor, the athletic commissioner, the matchmaker look at me, and call me over for the last check.

The Athletic Commissioner says, "We have the paperwork. Now we need your blood pressure checked." It's now about an hour before I am to fight.

The fight doctor says, "No that's not necessary. She's good." He looks at me and says, "She's fine. That's it. You can fight." I can see the Athletic Commissioner steaming. But he's looking ridiculous at this point.

I'd say. If there was an age discrimination in the fight terms, someone just violated that one. I found out later that one of the officials who had never fought and since I was older than he. And he thought that I shouldn't be able too. I thought, *'Oh men with little dicks, and no balls.'*

Phil was sitting with me and he said, "Jody, this is the calmest I've ever seen you. You have acted like a real professional fighter. I am proud of you."

I replied, "Thank you Phil.'

Soon enough I was called to walk out into the cage. Phil said, "You know what to do."

I replied, "Yes."

Phil reiterated, "Just like practice."

We receive our instructions from the referee. And the first round began. I came across the cage and had a bit of a brain fart, as I threw. She held onto the cage with her one hand and went to through a kick. No one said anything. And most in the MMA world know that it is illegal to hold onto the cage at any time.

She had good take down skills, but her punches were flaky. So I was relaxed when I was on the ground. I was not scooting out the side properly. So she more or less just held me down. Then the round ended. It appeared that this happened every round. And again, in the end, she out performed me and gained the title with a decision.

I realized I was none too upset at all. Phil realized what we had been dealing with. And I played the game and now it was time to move onto higher bars.

Figure 15. Fight Poster First Pro-MMA Match

Chapter Thirty-Three
Pinkalicious (2013)

Soon everything for my pro debut is accepted. The monies confirmed, travel and expenses are to be paid for. Contracts are signed. Phil says, "Jody, the next five weeks it will be *hell*. I will put you through *hell* every day you walk in here. You will spar with me."

Phil added, "I'll send you a video."

After I received the video and watched it, I told Phil the next day, "You know what her name is? *Pinkalicious*."

Phil smirked. I nearly always came up with a nickname for all my opponents. "Is it the hair?"

I replied, "No. You wouldn't know this, you never had little girls around you to raise. There's a cute little children's book our children have. It's titled, '*Pinkalicious*'. And I swear, the kid on the cover looks just like my opponent. It's hilarious man."

I nod, knowing he wants to see what I can still take. Saturday, June 8th 2013 will be my fifth fight since February 23rd, 2013, my thirteenth fight (stand-up) since October 8th, 2010, not including my ground matches.

And then it began, I was at Phil's *Asylum Fight Gym*, Monday through Saturday, every day. I was running seventy miles a week or so. Monday's depending on my work schedule sometimes I'd have an easy noon class, pad work, otherwise I'd be working till six thirty at night and then go to Vlad's *Sambo* class. Then at eight o'clock, Phil's MMA class, then at some point towards the end of Vlad's class at times, Phil would get a pair of four ounce gloves from the bin and say, "Let's *move*."

I'd comply. One Monday I remember he kicked me so hard in the first five minutes landing hard on my right hip bursa. I snarled, yelped, and then attacked. The pain was ridiculous. Everyone heard me. I moved forward so fast, feeling at first like I had to drag my right leg, the pain had shot through my body.

On Tuesday's it was the lunch time session, I'd be sparring again. On Wednesday, again Vlad's class at seven o'clock at night then Phil's MMA class at eight o'clock again. I didn't know when Phil would have me spar him in the evening. But I knew it was coming.

Thursday's we'd *move* again. Friday late afternoons were our private sessions now. Phil would warm me up and then pick me apart, sparring me again. Saturdays, Phil would take me to task again this time in between two class sessions or at the end of one and into the hour break, between the two morning classes.

With seventeen days to go, I had fractured my left humerus, I could feel it and saw the bleed coming through. I'd fractured it in a similar place nearly five years before. My right lower arm had a bone contusion and that you could see the blood draining through the arm beneath the elbow, as well.

By the twelfth day out from the fight I had a small tear in my abdomen and a pectoralis tear on my left side of my chest. I felt that tear wrestling with a guy I wrestled with a lot. Jeff heard me shriek when I went to pull my left arm out of his guard one night. Jeff felt awful, like he'd done something wrong. I explained it wasn't him, it was that I was being pushed.

And Phil realized with twelve days out, my left arm couldn't handle his kicks anymore. And my torso was too banged up to handle him kneeing, or kicking me in the stomach and the chest. So he aimed better at the things that weren't damaged. The one thing he wondered probably was, *'what would make me quit?'*

Quite a number of times in those five weeks before my pro debut, as Phil would finish with sparring me. He'd say, "I don't know why I'm harder on you than I am with the guys." He'd be shaking his head.

I would respond, "Because I demand it. It's all I got. I *ain't* got no talent." Funny there were times he'd say that line and I'd be crawling to the fencing from the mats in the cage. My legs wilting as I struggled to drag my body up to step out of the cage. And Phil would walk out like nothing touched him.

People would watch our sparring quite often. Vlad would consider me a freak show. In the past many didn't see Phil and I, when we were in his basement gym. Now it was more public. Funny thing was, the older women who did kickboxing class some with their daughters were really curious at times. They would ask their instructor if they could take a break and watch what we were doing in the cage.

George Petronella would say, "You invented the *Cage Crawl.*" It was the many times I couldn't stand up from the leg kicks Phil would throw to my legs. I then could no longer stand up for about twenty to thirty seconds. I would keep moving forward on all fours for the attack. I refused to stop. I refused to let a minor debilitation that I saw as temporary to stop me. I had to show I was willing and able to conquer anything. No matter what, I'd rather be dead than quit.

Enzo said, "You fight with your face."

And Phil would repeat, "The guys say you fight with your face. There is no quit in you."

Soon it was time to recover and fly out to Denver, Colorado. I knew the girl was good. I knew people who wouldn't fight her. But I didn't care. People called up Phil and scolded him. They told him I'd get hurt or worse. Phil didn't let on to that till after the fight.

After we arrived, I got settled in. And soon it was off to the weigh-ins. We waited. Lacey Schuckman wasn't there yet. I had ran a few miles before and now I was hungry. Some told me, she didn't think I'd show. Actually the message I got, was others didn't think I'd show.

We were actually early. The Athletic Commissioner was very professional. Thank God. Time passed and I was told Lacey was still trying to lose weight. Phil was a little perturbed. Meanwhile the weigh-ins were about to start. The promoter walked over to Phil and said, "She's going to be a little heavy."

Phil walked over to me, "Jody, come here. I'm a little upset."

I follow Phil as he waves me to a back staging area, "What?"

Phil replies, "She's not going to make weight. You don't have to take this."

I responded, "Hey man, we are here. I *ain't* going anywhere. We're here let's do this."

Phil asks, "Are you sure?"

I replied, "Yes. *Com'on,* we came all the way out here."

Phil remarks, "Okay." Shaking his head, he turns back to me and says, "I'll get something a little extra for you."

I respond, "More steak."

Phil walks, I follow him. Then I sit down as he gets the promoter, takes him aside and tells him, "We'll take it." Phil is visibly nervous. I could care less. I just want steak.

Soon my opponent arrives. Phil says, "Did you see her?"

I replied, "Nope."

Phil continues, "She's dripping wet. She's been trying to drop weight right up until she walked in the door. She wasn't ready for you. She's got a pro-career and she wasn't ready for you."

I replied, "*Ohhh*, you mean she thought no way in *hec*, that I'd show up."

Then they call us up for weigh-ins after there is a ruckus about a previous girl fight weigh-in. This one woman was pissed, her opponent was heavier, didn't apparently make weight, and she was fuming.

Then I step on the scale. I weigh-in at 103.3 pounds. *Pinkalicious* steps on the scale weighing over 109 pounds. I pay no attention to it. The Athletic Commissioner is cool with it, because I was fine with it. I wanted the fight. It was for 105 pounds and the main event. *Pinkalicious* (Lacey Schuckman) is a huge name. Ranked top five in the world, I'm told.

Then fight morning arrives. It was a beautiful sunny Denver day, mild out. All sorts of thoughts race through my head. I'm out of mind scared. Although this is normal for me in any type of event I've ever done. This time it feels more intense, bigger. I call Phil after I go for my morning fight run to meditate and have my conversation with God.

Phil can hear my nervousness in my voice. "I just gotta talk, like. You know?"

Phil replies, "I'll meet you in the lobby."

I respond, "Okay thanks. I want a scone and a latte. Or something I'm familiar with. Okay?"

Phil soon arrives in the lobby and we meet and go find a familiar coffee brand shop I like. I say, "Phil, I'm like out of mind scared. Like you know? I can't explain it. Help me mentally with this."

Phil responds, "Jody, that's healthy. It's good."

I replied, "Okay, I needed to know that. It's the most intense I can remember before any athletic event in my life."

Before we know it, it's now afternoon and time to get to the event site for the fight. We warm me up a little. We check out the cage when it's quiet before anyone is really around. It's still about seven hours before the fight. We are the main event. She's very popular.

Then I get called to take a pregnancy test. The doctor instructs me how to use this over the counter pregnancy test. I have a brain-fart and ask him again. I giggle and say, "How would you know, young man?" We smile, I go into the ladies room and take the test. I passed, and I didn't have to study neither.

Time passes, Phil is gradually getting me warmed up, yet not too much so I can save my energy. The feeling is different this time. I'm actually relaxed, even in my usual jittery nervousness before an event.

Soon enough, *Still Unbroken* by *Lynyrd Skynard,* is playing. It's my walk out song. I nearly panic. There was so much noise we couldn't hear my name called. I yelled, "Phil now! They're playing my walk out song. We got to go."

Soon we are walking out to the cage. The cage was a smaller size than I'd remembered and then imagined in my mind's eye. Yet, I think it was due to the way the place where this event was being held was now packed with people. The roof of the club was open. The balconies, the floor, and every place there could be even standing room was packed. I looked quickly up, around, and I couldn't begin to calculate how many people were present.

Soon the referee has me in the cage and I'm awaiting my opponent. As she arrived, the crowd cheered. I looked back at Phil as the referee checked her in her corner. Phil said loudly, "Just like practice!" I nodded. I felt fine. It was amazing all the injury I had just before-hand, it's all gone. Not a tweak. Not till a day after the fight anyway.

Then it was *'go time'*. I galloped across the cage. I got to her corner to strike first. As I threw a cross, she threw a head kick with her left leg. I blocked it simultaneously with my right arm, as I threw my straight left punch.

Evidently, we went to strike each other at the same time. I felt a sort of push to my left, yet was on automatic pilot to just throw leather. Unknown to me, when Phil saw her launch the head kick. He thought, 'Oh no.' Figuring, I would get knocked out. He told me later. That he couldn't believe I actually was able to block the head kick with my arm as I punched with the other arm.

I couldn't gain my balance but yet I was still trying to operate throwing punches. She seemed to lose her balance falling forward, the kick got me off balance enough where I was falling backwards as she was falling forwards.

Then as I landed on my back, she ended up in perfect mount position. I was relaxed. Some punches came down, but I was so relaxed, I didn't feel them. I felt in my realm.

I was used to this position in the first round. I didn't mind it. That became a problem that I was too relaxed where I didn't even feel how fast she rolled into an arm-bar position with my left arm, and snagged it well. I had to tap.

Under a minute and she got me in an arm-bar. I felt bad. I was disappointed. And I felt bad I didn't get to give her more of a fight. She may have been relieved. We got up. I thanked her and hugged her. She did as well. I apologized for not making the fight last longer. Fighters just love to fight, they can't help it. We all love to win, but to win you have to accept the fight first.

Figure 16. First Pro MMA Fight for me. Pinkalicious wins.

Figure 17. Colorado Post-Fight June 8th, 2013, Lacey and Jody.

Chapter Thirty-Four
The Next Frontier (2014)

Over the past year, as Phil Dunlap was training me. He warmed me up as usual. He hadn't tested me in a while. In the beginning of 2013 he knew we were going to take me from amateur MMA to the pro-MMA level.

I'd been under Phil's tutelage since June 4th. 2008. First for self-defense. Then by the end of March 2009, we began to focus on fighting for competition. So here we were, after my first pro MMA fight. It was around the end of July 2013. The gym was quiet.

It was a Friday afternoon private lesson with Phil. Ethan Gomes came in as we finished our warm-up. Two others were in the gym. Phil says, "You wanna *move* a little?"

I never said, 'No' to Phil. I nodded and said, "Yeah."

Anyone who really has been trained by Phil knows that the question he asked really meant; 'Are you ready to be tested?' So as Phil gets a sip of water, and finds a pair of four ounce gloves to wear in a bin nearby. As usual, I begin to pray that God protects me, heals me, and gives me courage. Enough seconds pass by, that I start to say my third prayer in a mantra form.

I know Phil will pick me apart. He knows even though I can take hits to the head. He will aim for what can suck the life out of my physical body. He and the guys have known I quite often fight with my face. But if you were to punch my liver area over and over again, eventually I will tire. And if you punch and kick my thighs a bunch as Phil often does; eventually I will stumble. However, I will always attempt to move forward. I've learned that from long distance running and from living life. That no matter how much anything hurts, just keep moving. It will get no worse.

So here we were ready to begin. Phil and I enter the cage. Many who know me, know that I don't usually touch gloves in my fights. Why? Before the fight you are the enemy. Then, after the fight most times you can be my friend. I treat Phil's sparring me, like a real match or even a real street fight. I am not allowed to stop. I must not drop my hands. I must fight back. I must move forward and try to take angles. I must be aggressive. I make him tell me when *it's* over.

No matter how I think I might be failing, I can not let him intimidate me. I must show something or attempt something new he's worked on with me. I remember only twice in all these sessions did Phil stop me prematurely. One time I was coming off an illness, he really felt I wasn't ready. It took all he had to keep me from feeling ashamed.

The second time it occurred my nose broke so badly upon his strike to my face he thought he broke my cheek bone as well   He later stated he felt something give to his fist from my face. No blood was coming out of my nose or mouth. I was too busy absorbing the pain. Keeping my hands up. I remained standing, trying to blink my eyes open. I was temporarily blinded as both eyes were tearing up. I knew to move forward for I wanted to show, *'no matter what I was still in the game'*.

As the pain seared through the forehead and into the top of my scalp; I moved forward saying, "I can do this. Give me a chance."

He stops, and says, "Jody, get down." At this point I begin to see him partially out of my right eye and see his hands are down at his sides. I don't want to give in, the searing pain was fleeting, I was fine.

I responded, "Hey, I'm good. I can't stop. What if this really happens?"

Phil repeats himself, "Jody. No get to the ground. Now!"

Still holding my hands to my face, I answer, "But why? I can try. Give me a second." I started to be able to see more.

He repeats again, Jody, just get down now!" Phil sounds a little panicked.

I reply, "Really?." The panic in Phil's voice was not something I was familiar with.

He continues, "Jody, you broke your nose. Get down."

I reply, "Gee, I felt burning through my head. Well, okay then. I'm not tasting blood." I slowly get down on all fours. Then blood comes flying out of my nose and mouth as I deny a broken nose.

I then hear Phil say, "Oh. Thank God." As he runs to the bathroom to get paper-towels. Blood is in a puddle on the mat and I realize, *gee I guess I broke it again.*

Phil comes back with the paper-towels. He begins to clean up. I felt a little spinning. Tons of my blood was displayed all around me yet, mostly in front of me. "Yeah, I guess I broke my nose. Can you put it back on for me?"

The guys in the gym continue training. In a hilarious neurotic essence as only Phil could display cleaning up a fighter's blood off the floor. Phil says, "If you didn't bleed like that Jody, I felt like I broke your cheek bone."

I responded, "Yeah I know what I did wrong, too."
I continue to explain what I felt I did wrong. "I actually saw me doing it wrong. I tilted my head forward and down as I threw my cross. I went too slow with the punch too. I've been trying to correct myself. Now I understand it. I lacked confidence that's why I did it wrong. I wanted to perfect my stance as I threw the punch and was actually so aware of screwing up. So, I looked down to check my stance."

I laughed, "I won't do that again."

So now nearly three years later, July 2013 we begin to spar, as Ethan Gomes sits atop the cage to watch. Ethan joins us about fifteen minutes into the sparring. I know I'm screwing up on taking angles. However, I'm moving better. I'm blocking a lot of Phil's shots. He's now throwing knees to my chest. I block a bunch of knees.

Phil comments, "Good".

At some point during this I ask as we move, "Taking angles?"

I hear a blurb, "Yeah." Then *whack*. I went to the left instead of going to the right. He's landed a nice solid leg kick to my right thigh. I snarl as I am annoyed with myself.

After I block some of the entourage of shots, Phil quickly grabs me behind my neck with both his gloved hands into a clinch. His left knee lands spot on, up into the liver. I'm feeling pain shoot through me. It shoots through to my right scapulae. I'm fighting my body heading to the ground.

I fall. I get up. I fall. I get up. I repeat this process of falling and getting up eight times. Finally, I'm standing, my body shaking, moving no more than the six inches I've stumbled to. As I go to move forward through nausea and pain. I hear Ethan, "Wow. That hurt me." I'm in too much pain to reciprocate a comedic gesture. As the pain and nausea lingers, we continue.

About a minute or so later I get my energy back. I'm still nausea, but less so. And my right side calms down. Phil ends the sparring session after twenty-five minutes.

Chapter Thirty-Five
Dismayed (2014)

As Both Phil and I went away with our families. He with Lorraine and his step-sons. And I with Norman and our two daughters. Unknown to us our lives would become altered.

Phil and I were back in his not even a year old *Asylum Fight Gym*. He told me he hurt his left arm on vacation. Phil is holding pads for me and it doesn't look happy. I ask, "Hey, Phil you're really hurting aren't you?"

Phil replies, "Uh yeah. You want to just take a look at my arm?"

I start to walk over and say, "What'd yah do?"

Phil responds, "I was para-sailing and I fell on this part of the arm." Phil points to the mid-humerus part at the deltoid tuberosity.

I get my right hand to touch the spot and within one inch of Phil's arm I feel a void of energy. "Uh, that's damaged. How's you sugar? Something is with your pancreas. You better cool it on the soda. I can't diagnose, but it feels broken to me. The energy has a void."

Phil responds, "Yeah, I'm going to see the doctor. It feels broken."

I replied, "You alright to do this? You know, you need me to make you a kale and apple drink every day."
Phil rolls his eyes, "Oh God."

I respond, "Oh *com'on*. Just try it. Yah pussy."

That week, Phil gets his left arm and shoulder checked. He tells me, "They wanted to immobilize me. I have a torn labrum, an avulsion fracture of the deltoid area, and some other tears. I'm seeing another doctor."

I respond, "Oh boy. Don't immobilize. Get another opinion. Stop the soda."

Later Phil calls me, as I'm driving to the bank. I pull over my minivan to answer the phone. "Hello."

Phil asks, "Jody, its Phil. Do you have a really good shoulder guy?"

I respond, "As a matter of fact I do. He's the best. And he won't cut you if you don't want that. He does believe in therapy." I proceed to give Phil his name and town he is in. "Just tell him who you are. What you do. And that you'll rehab it." Phil agrees.

Meanwhile Phil's pancreas is starting to really erupt. He sees the shoulder doctor I recommended. The doctor although a surgeon, agrees with how Phil wants to handle his shoulder and arm. Writes Phil a prescription for his injury for Physical Therapy, and nothing else as

Phil had desired. As that issue was getting treated. He
was starting to feel really sick.

As he dove into more medical issues, now with his
pancreas. Two doctors told him he had pancreatic
cancer. When he told me this. I responded with, "How
would they know that?" Phil shrugged. I continued,
"How did you fill out those medical forms when you
went into their offices? You didn't put your family
history down did you?"

Phil responded, "Ohhhh."

I replied, "You gave them the diagnosis. They're
running all the way to the bank with it, buddy. Let me
get you a third opinion."

I did the research and found a world-renowned
pancreatic cancer specialist. I then read up on him. He
was from Thailand. Yet, his office was close by. I then
contacted a few doctors who I knew. They all said,
'He's the *go to* doctor they'd take their mothers to.'

I called Phil up and sent Lorraine the information.
They got an appointment quickly. I gave them a
reference name, just in case they needed a little help to
get in quicker.

Finally, after a few months of pain, illness,
misdiagnosis, and lack of proper treatment. Phil and
Lorraine now found out that Phil did not have pancreatic
cancer.

Phil had pancreatitis and there were cysts more or less
bursting on his pancreas, which pained him greatly. This
was caused by a dental debacle, where years before Phil

had apparently been overdosed on a very strong antibiotic without any probiotics given and thus developing CDIF. And now it was wrecking him. Taking him down. He had to give up his *Mountain Dew*.

I can say it was a nice 2014 New Year's present. But the war was not over. Just as Phil was getting better news on his arm and shoulder seemed to be healing a bit as well. We had set up my second pro MMA fight in February 2014 in Florida. I had to go for medicals.

I went to a medical clinic of people I knew. I couldn't get into see my regular internist fast enough and I needed a brain scan and eye exams. I had a friend who had a clinic and the hours were perfect. They kept the cost low as well. I paid out of pocket.

Everything seemed fine. The last thing I would have thought, was that my scan of my head would've come back with a problem. I got a phone call from the doctor who'd examined me. I had a growth in my face. She sent me all the reports and scan with the report as well. She said, "You need to take care of this."

My friend hand-delivered it to me at my office, he said, "I'm sorry." This went from, 'I want to win for Phil'. To... 'Am I going to see our daughters graduate from high school?' I didn't have the heart to tell my husband first. So I practiced on Phil. Which of course was easier than telling my husband. Phil told Lorraine and she did some research.

I contacted a few doctors I knew through my business and didn't let them know it was me. I just asked questions. Told them the first diagnosis. Two of them said, "It's got to come out."

The third one said, "Let me send you information on this type of growth."

He sent me a ton of material. And it read quite clearly that if it was not completely removed that the part that was left, even if not malignant had a high chance of becoming malignant after an unsuccessful full removal.

The growth sat on the left trigeminal nerve, measuring the size in width, height and depth of a quarter. The clinic doctor followed up and sent me for second scan with contrast. She called me and urged me to go. "You have to move on this. Aren't you having symptoms?" She began to name them.

I replied, "*ahh* I'm fine." She sounded incredibly perplexed. I thanked her, and we said 'good-bye'. I sat back in my office and knew I'd had symptoms. I thought it was hormonal due to my age, as if menopause was occurring. Yet I also knew I was a *DES* (Diethylstilbestrol) *daughter*. I also knew in the past, my gynecologists had put me on a pill for eleven years that caused a high rate of cancer in DES daughters. I also had a relative die of a brain tumor at age thirty-seven. My brother died of a growth crushing his heart and valves at age forty-five.

I can recall nights at home when I'd stand in front of my 270 pound water bag punching it for an hour or two or more. Nothing would occur. One night I threw 30,000 punches with my four ounce gloves on. I was elated for two hours, two minutes and thirty-six seconds. I had not a symptom.

Then the next night at eight thousand punches, then it would happen. I'd feel like I was watching a *Batman and Robin* series, my world would tilt for apparently no reason at all. Then that would clear, and then I'd feel like I was sinking two or three feet into the rugged floor beneath me. Those were two of the symptoms, forms of vertigo, she had described. And the pressure I felt building in my face, felt like someone left an elbow in my face where the trigeminal nerve would be.

I knew enough about the position of the growth and what the trigeminal nerve controls. I'd had clients with severe trigeminal neuralgia. Some it effected the plantaris muscle in their legs. The muscle it apparently effects, runs from behind the lower hamstring, through the back of the knee, and down the posterior portion of the leg attaching into the foot.

A couple clients had it snap on them, and they were on crutches for six months after. Yes, the nerve is one of our twelve cranial nerves, but it could reek havoc on other areas of the body. That's the good part about me, and the regular job I've had since age thirty. I must know my anatomy and physiology.

Finally, I told my husband, after I spoke with another friend whom I could trust in the medical field. She was in the alternative medical field. She felt it probably wouldn't grow that fast, due to the nature of that type of growth. However, I knew it wasn't there before. I'd had other scans in the last four years and it wasn't on them. I had all the scans and the paperwork on them too.

When I told my husband, I was now calm and it was quiet, the children were sleeping. He said, "Jody, what would you normally have the inclination to do? Wouldn't you go to Ken?"

I replied, "Yes. And pray."

Norman remarked, "Then I say, do what you're comfortable with."

I replied, "Thank you. I'll have people pray for me and see Ken."

After that I was relieved. Over the next week I made two appointments with Ken Andes. And a man of the cloth walked into my office whom I knew. I asked for prayers. And then a woman I knew, who was a Eucharistic Minister came in the same week. I told her and she said, "Right now. Let's do this right now." She did her prayers and rituals with me and she said, "You're going to be fine. I just know it."

Three weeks later, I felt better. The pressure from my face was gone. It was gone for the first time in about eight months.

Soon three months passed, all the symptoms I had were gone. Prayers and two acupuncture treatments and I was healed. Unfortunately, the Florida Athletic Commissioner was the one who would not let me fight in February 2014 fight card.

However, I got an offer to do another exhibition match in April. And pulled it off just two weeks before Phil lost his gym. Phil was still unhealthy with his pancreatitis, he was financially drained to the point of bankruptcy. He lost his regular job in November 2013. The position that Phil held was in sales. Which in the aspect of sales he was in, was very unpredictable.

Phil always worked a regular job since I'd known him, and also taught people and trained them self-defense and fighting as well. Besides he handled the full financial load of the new gym, never mind the management as well, then training people to boot.

So here I was knowing Phil was in trouble physically, emotionally, and financially. I did whatever I could to ease his worries. I was glad he was with Lorraine and her boys. He needed them and how.

We were getting ready for an amateur MMA fight night in the city. Three of our amateur fighters were on the card. It was for Friday, April 25th 2014 in Manhattan. It was a beautiful night. I told Phil I would help where ever he needed me. I'd helped Phil work the corner enough before in MMA, Muay Thai and Boxing matches. This was 'old hat'.

At the same time, no one knew Phil was losing the gym. I did. The doors would be locked forever on Tuesday April 29th 2014. I protected Phil, I knew what he was going through. I said nothing. It was nobodies' business.

When he left that night with Lorraine after the fights were over. I had a feeling we'd not see Phil at the *Asylum Fight Gym* again. That chapter was over. What was to come, I had no clue. I worried some. I wanted him to know that I knew he did his best. And that was all I'd ever expect from anyone. But he was alive, and that's what mattered.

No one would know if I'd ever get another pro fight ever again. But I didn't want to let go. I wasn't done.

Figure 18. Karl's place in Las Vegas 2015

Chapter Thirty-Six
"I'll Take It" (2014)

People have asked me why I answer, "I'll take it." As a gut reaction to a fight opportunity about ninety-nine percent of the time, even when I don't know the details of the opponent. It is because I want to fight.

I had calculated by early 2014, I'd had about eighty-six fights offered, three of the offers I had to turn down due to me having an illness or an injury. Of the fights (stand-up involved=fights) that came to fruition by that time, twelve fights had come to fruition. Seventy one of the fights, were either the other party said, 'yes', then backed out. Or they were no where to be found after saying, 'yes'. Or they were injured and there was no replacement to be found for me in time. Or they found replacements, and the replacement(s) would say, 'yes', then later a 'no' would come from their camp.

There were fights where we had anywhere from two to four replacements for a fight occurring, only for the whole thing to fall through and I wouldn't have that fight. There were plenty of times these fights would fall apart at a point right down at the wire.

On April 29th 2014, my coach, trainer, manager, and friend Phil, lost his gym. Most thought, including Phil and my husband, Norman that I'd stop fight training. What many didn't realize was, I was addicted to fighting and the training that went with it. It was still new to me, and I couldn't get enough of it.

I didn't want to throw away Phil's training. It was sacred to me. The whole experience was unique. I felt it would never be taught to me or anyone else quite like that again.

Yet I realized I could re-adapt Phil's training. If I was flexible and his training was as good as I thought it was. I could re-adapt to any format of fighting. Due to my personality I could re-adapt to any coach, as well. It was because I love taking orders. I like to come through when it's not expected of me or doesn't seem attainable.

I pride myself on getting through muck and mire. I've always been a *mudder*. In contrast, in my life I have learned early of my own insignificance. Knowing that at such a young age, diminishes your ego. So being, knowing everyone else is just as important as you are. You must help everyone else, where you can. Why? Because, they are as lively, and possible as you are.

In knowing this, when my friend's health, divorce, and finances came tumbling down on him. I knew I had to show Phil, that all he did with me, and taught me were of great significance. I felt at the very least, I owed him that respect. So, I willingly 'soldiered on'.

Phil hoping I would keep fighting. He also wanted people who felt displaced to have a place to go and continue their dreams and aspirations. Phil searched as he was financially bankrupt, emotionally torn and not the man he desired to be. He thought about other people. As was usual many times for Phil. No matter the circumstances.

Phil went to a number of martial art and fight gyms. I looked for places and so did my friend, Peter. We kept our eyes peeled for Phil to have the *group-ons* fulfilled and fighters satisfied. Due to the economy, Phil found it was not always easy to find a good deal with scrupulous owners.

Finally, a week or so after the gym closed, Phil once again met with another gym owner. It was five minutes up the road from the old gym. How perfect. Phil met with the owner, Rafael Melendez. Rafael, a retired New York City Police Officer, worked the Bronx and also was from the Bronx originally. Rafael just opened up his dojo, *Amerikick* the year before.

Rafael, a no non-sense guy. He'd been a fighter as well. He had title belts. As a matter of fact his cousins also held titles in Boxing, Judo, and Ju-Jitsu also. Rafael, per Phil was willing to train me.
Phil was there Mondays and Wednesday nights till Wednesday, June 4th 2014. That date marked Phil and my six year anniversary of him training me to the day.

I fought that Saturday, June 7th 2014. However, the Monday, June 2nd, 2014, before the fight night I found out Phil was taking a job out in Las Vegas, Nevada. Phil and I had the discussion on Thursday, May 29th, 2014. I knew he really had to take that job out there to gain health, and get out of bankruptcy.

I quickly decided that Monday night, June 2nd to make an impression. I was to fight two Muay Thai fights in the same night June 7th, in upstate New York. I love to fight. So, the idea sat well with me. Yet, I also knew I was doing the promoter a favor. I was to have a 105 pound fight, which is my true fight weight as the first fight of the night.

My second fight was to be about two hours later, fight number thirteen or fourteen on the fight card. The second fight would be at 145 pounds and also a Muay

Thai Fight as well. The 145 pound girl lost her opponent last minute and she'd sold many tickets. I'd stepped up many times before to fill in. Phil called me, 'The Relief Pitcher.'

Time passed June 7th came. I had Phil and Rafael both in my corner. Mark Jacobs, a sports writer, who I'd trained with, came to cheer me on. The 105 pound Muay Thai fight was constantly being changed.

Finally, an hour before the show, one of the promoters came to me and said, "Jody, you got one fight." I sighed. The last minute up and downs had been so stressful, which seemed to change just that day about four times, was getting tiring.

He continued, "145 pounds is your fight." I was relieved. At least I had now had time to rest, eat and drink. And I could reset my brain to a permanent thought. He continued, "You're at the end of the night."

I saw my opponent. She was bigger. One of her legs was twice the size of one of mine in diameter at the thigh. I only had learned how to check kicks that week. I was use to absorbing them, because in the past I lacked balance.

I'd began to work on balance drills as well. I also had just learned how to kick in the past week for the same reason. From the time I can remember I had balance issues. The fear of standing on one leg was now slowly diminishing. This fight would force me to use what I just learned. The opponent had been doing Muay Thai for years. I was a brawler. I wanted to put on a good

323

show. I wanted to appease the promoter and both coaches.

That night I lost to a decision. The one thing I knew was I didn't cower, and I should've kicked more.

As Phil, Rafael, Mark and I exited the stage area, the promoter was laughing, put his hand on his heart, shaking his head. He said, "You killed me. You scared the crap out of me." Then he thanked us. We walked down to the basement staging area, sat down for a second. Rafael had to get going. It was a long night indeed. Especially for him.

We said our 'good-byes' to Rafael. Then the three of us, Phil, Mark and myself sat down in the plastic chairs provided. All of us slumping, as we sighed in tandem.

I then said smiling, "Wild, Huh?"

Phil asked, "What?"

I repeated, "Wild. She was big."

He responded, "She weighed in at 143 pounds hours before the fight."

Mark begins to chuckle. I replied, "Yep, and five or so hours later 148 pounds with me in the cage at 104 pounds. You know what? I think I actually kicked, and I didn't fall over."

Smiling Mark said, "Yeah. And you actually improved. You look more like a fighter now."

I responded, "Hey, I even checked some kicks."

Phil responded, "Yep. I counted three or four." We laughed. Phil continued shaking his head, "Man, every time in between rounds I kept saying to myself, 'I can't believe I put a mouse in the cage with an elephant.'"

Mark and I laughed harder.

I asked, "It was that much of a difference visually? Huh?" As Mark was still chuckling.

Phil says, "Jody, did you see her thighs?"

I respond, "Well Yeah, but I figured maybe they'd make her tired. Like she'd wear them out on me."

Soon enough we packed up and left. I thanked Mark. Then Phil and I walked out to our cars together. Phil was parked near me. We chatted a bit.

I said to Phil before departing, "Uh, do me a favor. Tell Rafael before you leave… 'Tell it to the Marine', cause she'll listen and do her best." Phil nodded. I continued, "Rafael needs to know that about me."

After that I knew I might see Phil one more time before he headed west. I got in my car, Phil got in his car. Phil left. My phone rang, it was Rafael. We chatted. I hoped I hadn't disappointed Rafael. Then after that, I left the parking garage and headed home. It was way past midnight.

The next week I worked on re-formatting my thinking. I fought off uneasy feelings, mostly of sadness, some of confusion. Yet being grateful knowing Phil would be better off. And albeit, I was forced to land new coaches. I'd landed on my feet, attaining a Boxing/MMA coach at first, who one of the guys I knew from the *Asylum fight Gym*. Then a trainer, MMA coach and manager, whom Phil had paired me up with in a gym that was Rafael.

My friend Peter Dell'Orto, stuck by me as we worked out our schedules, so we could keep training three to four times a week together,

Time passed, and as usual some wondered what drove me. I wondered too. I just couldn't get rid of the fight. The desire to fight, that is. At times, I had feelings of severe callousness. Very rarely did I ever experience these feelings like this in the past. I wondered what they meant. Was it that I matured as a person or as a fighter or both? Was it a form of self-protection? Or was it fear?

One thing I knew I couldn't discuss this with anyone. It was too deep. And no one that was new in my fight life could I have this discussion with. Phil perhaps would have been the one for this discussion. He knew my guts.

So I asked myself, '*what made me happy*? *What made me driven*?' The answers were more enriching. Besides, taking orders. I enjoy having the opportunity to motivate people. And if the presence of my drive is strong enough. People who want to learn or become fighters will make me push them.

I will do things not expected of me. Yes, I love to achieve. But even better, I enjoy seeing others achieve.

If I can push them by pushing myself. Then everybody wins. That is some of what makes me happy. Even better is being of great use. That drives me. It usually makes me happy.

As time had passed. I needed to know I was still a fighter. After a couple of respites due to injury and illness. I realized very few coaches would ever really give me a chance. I still needed to fight.

Eventually, I hung out and sparred with Ray, who tried to put something together. But it wasn't the same. I left both the Boxing/MMA coach and the gym owner/coach that Phil had introduced me to. Due to the fact neither were really into me fighting.

I had one bad match after four girls turned me down for a title fight in Muay Thai in the Bronx, which I was not really trained completely in, nor was it going to be my forte. The coach and gym owner Phil knew let me know publicly he didn't think much of Mixed Martial Arts. I was a bit shocked. Soon afterwards I left him. No ill words, after eight months I just walked out one day. I didn't go back.

Soon about four weeks later in late February, early March of 2015, I decided to take our oldest daughter away to go visit Phil.

She wanted to say she'd been to Las Vegas. But also she loved summer. She also was interested in some of the ground fighting I knew. She hadn't missed a day of school at that point since pre-K, and here it was, she was in sixth grade at age twelve.

She had always had straight 'A's' pretty much all her years of school so far. So I would treat her to one day off of school, we would have a quick weekend excursion, like Mommy and Me time.

Just before I flew out there, Phil got clearance from his doctors that he could train fully again in his fighting.

Figure 19. Karl's 2015 Phil working pads with Jody.

Chapter Thirty-Seven
She Broke Karl's Wall...Then the Car Door Hit Her... (2015)

...In the face. It was near the end of February 2015. I was recovered from all injuries I'd had in the past. I got a flight for myself and our oldest daughter, Sarah to fly out to Las Vegas. It was only for a couple days to visit Phil, relax with our oldest daughter, train and have Phil test me. She needed a respite, and I wanted to show Phil I was still a fighter. And besides I missed Phil, and the essence of his style of training me. No one really seemed to know how to treat me as a fighter.

We flew out late Thursday night. A snow storm was to hit that Sunday morning, March 1st, 2015. The storm was to arrive back home when we were supposed to return back east. I threw caution to the wind. We both needed a break.

By the time Sarah and I landed in Las Vegas and I rented a car it was past ten at night on our drive to Phil and Lorraine's home from the airport. Phil waited up for us. The two of us got there, and the feeling was so much like when you haven't seen your favorite relatives for years. Where you walk in the door, they've been waiting up for you, and everyone has passed out but one and the dog.

So Phil and Bella the dog were up. Sarah was relaxed and we just plopped our stuff down, hugged. We had water, Sarah fell asleep in my lap on the couch with Bella, as Phil and I talked. We could've talked forever, it seemed. But I was passing out and so was Phil.

Hours later I was up, cleaned, and went out for an eight mile run. Oh, that warmth from the Las Vegas sun was so welcoming. My body had been so pained and rigid, I hadn't recognized the usual damp cold of our winters back east. I was distracted in toughing it out to keep my fighting alive. I didn't know how much my body was contracted. The muscles melted as I ran in the desert that day.

I thought to myself, '*Norman would really be enjoying this. Now I know why my buddy Jim moved out to Utah.*'

I got back and everybody was up. Phil said, "Hey around noon, we will head over to Karl's. Okay?"

I replied, "Absolutely."

I double-checked with Lorraine and Sarah. I knew Sarah would be fine. I told Sarah, "No pool, till I get back. You've got reading, Bella and TV. I'll take you to get your nails done after we hike, and get a late lunch." She was good with it.

Soon enough it was time to head over to Karl's. So Phil and I left through his gated community and drove a bit and then through another gated community where Karl resided.

We arrived at Karl's. He answered the door. As we entered, you could see Karl made a little gym from a step away from his home's foyer. He used an extra open room to our left before the family room about thirteen feet away diagonally. To our immediate right were steps going up.

We shook hands, and chatted a bit. Then Phil had me do some pad work. I hadn't done this kind of work in eight months. Everyone had handled me differently. Peter handled me the closest from I had worked with Phil in such work. Peter and I were the two that I actually realized, stuck together on a regular basis after the gym closed. Peter and I trained together at least twice a week, sometimes three times a week after Phil's gym had closed, and Phil had moved.

Then next thing I hear is, "You want to *move?*"

I know what's coming. And, *'he wants to know what's left in the tank. Does he still have a fighter in me?'*

He knows I must work this, to show I want to continue even now to fight competitively. We've been through injury and illness in the same state and separately. "Yeah. Sure." I replied.

Now an outsider who'd never seen Phil pick me apart, and maybe never seen a woman crazed in fight would witness the style of Phil training me and of my response to the training. These were rare moments. Not many from the outside have witnessed this. It has freaked quite a few people out. We made a young woman cry once. And some men shook their heads. But they weren't real fighters.
As we spar and Phil does his job. My hand discipline is good, Phil let's me know. Then he kicks me hard in the chest and I fly back against one of the walls in Karl's

332

little gym. I felt the pain of my back slamming against the lower portion of the wall. The one thing I know is when I get hit hard, I make sure I get back up, and fast. That mentality began when I was four years old. It's my form of acting as though nothing has occurred.

I popped up off the ground and off the wall. And I saw Karl out of the corner of my right eye attempt to come over, and find out if I was okay. Karl asked, "Are you Okay?" I was up on the attack aimed at Phil, as Karl was speaking. I remained focused. When Phil, and I finished. We checked the wall. I broke a piece of Karl's wall with my back. I never felt anything afterwards. No worse for the wear.

Phil said, "You did good."

I was relieved. The tiger was still in the tank. Later that day, after Sarah and I relaxed back at Phil and Lorraine's. Phil said, "We will go easy tonight at Karl's."

That night as we went to get into the car with Sarah to get to Karl's seven o'clock class. The sky was so beautiful. I looked up and as I looked down, I whacked the corner of my right eye with the corner of Phil's car door as it swung out of my hand in slow motion.

Phil said, "Are you okay?" Then came over and he took me inside and looked at me. And he had to explain to Lorraine what just happened in the driveway, "You look okay." A bit concerned, Phil went and got me an ice pack. Then off we went. No bad damage. I now had two black eyes in one day.

We did ground that night with Karl. Sarah trained with two little boys, Karl's children are Chinese and Dutch/German. And another little Asian boy was there. They were near Sarah's size. She enjoyed herself doing a form of Jiu Jitsu.

The next day, we went to Karl's again, and they were belt testing in Kempo. Three men were getting tested. I fought two of the one's getting tested for their test. Then I fought Kyle, Lorraine's sixteen year old six foot four inch son, whom Phil had been training.

Then Phil wanted to '*move*' again with me. I could tell my whole body was wiped. I realized that I could barely absorb as much as I had the day before. I have no clue how many minutes I'd sparred just before for the belt testing with stand up and ground, against three men. Never mind, Phil taking me to task the day before.

Soon our little visit ended. But I knew that I was still in the fight game and soon I would get another professional MMA fight.

As time passed and I remained training with Peter two to three times a week. Both our schedules got tighter. I would train here and there with different people. Killer Ken and George I trained with them in the spring of 2016 here and there, when they could meet me in New City, New York.

I really needed to fight. However, soon after my mother-in-law got more ill and then subsequently died. I trained distracted, worried about my husband. Then I lost two friends. One my husband and I treasured and was around till he moved the end May 2014 out to Utah.

Jim died around April 12th 2016. By then Jim was the fourth person that I knew who'd died in 2016 already, with the year not even half over.

Again, I was offered fights when I had to take care of family, money was low. The upside of the first four months of that year was my CT Scan of my head and physical thereafter. The growth was completely gone, now two years later. It vanished. I'd almost forgotten about it, since the symptoms had retreated within three months of a bad CT Scan of my head in January 2014.

I then received a call from Phil about a fight in Danbury. I was up for it. But I needed a corner man. And I needed someone who knew hands, and who also knew Phil and I. The fight was mid-July 2016. I got George Petronella to corner me. I knew he was a reliable guy. He was from our old basement gym and had fought for Phil in the past.

Then I needed a Boxing gym to train. I called Phil, "There's this boxing gym. A guy I met twice, seems nice, Joe Rossi. You know the name?"

Phil responded, "Perfect."

I called Joe on May 27th 2016, we set aside time at night to speak on the phone, Sunday, May 29th 2016. We spent about forty-five minutes on the phone. And on Tuesday, May 31st, 2016, I entered the YESS gym. I was offered other fights out west, yet I didn't have the money to travel. Even though I'm a professional MMA fighter, promotions don't always foot the bill to bring fighters out. 2016 was a rough financial year. However,

335

fighting more locally I had the offer in mid-May for July 2016 fight.

I won the July 2016 match by decision against a young woman age thirty. As this book goes to press, I keep training awaiting another offer.

Over time I have had people imply or ask when I would retire. I can say when I first started this fighting stuff, I thought I'd be done after a couple years. However, I can say I'm so in love with fighting that I have no clue.

I recognize as I had in the beginning that I feel like a infant in the sport of fighting. And like a child, in the joy of being able to partake in the sport of fighting.

And at the end of the day, as I discover what else I can learn.

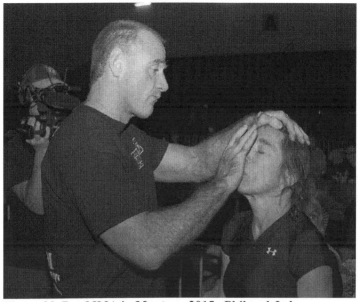

Figure 20. Pro MMA in Montana 2015. Phil and Jody.

Epilogue
"You Got Nothing."…Except Faith

As I still maintain my love for running and fighting. Right now I am training and awaiting opportunities to fight. I have always loved Boxing and am now training in Dumont, New Jersey at Joe Rossi's Boxing and Barbell Gym, "YESS".

Trainer Mr. Steve Bratter, a well-versed Boxing trainer, '*old-school*' is currently training me. I've landed here, and feel it is my new fight home. I hope some day to attain the professional level of Boxing. I do not see an end any time soon.

I picture myself in my sixties, perhaps then, maybe I will attain enough knowledge in Boxing from the training staff of YESS, and Joe Rossi. So that I may help train people and help people reach the joy of competing in fighting as I have and do.

I still remain close friends with Phil Dunlap, who now resides and trains fighters out in Las Vegas, Nevada. There were times in Phil's old Basement Gym and in the new *Asylum Fight Gym*, before that closed, someone would say, "You got nothing." Usually, when they said this. I'd have a submission or a dominant position on them. Yes, they would be bigger, stronger, and faster. Yet, I had faith in what Phil instructed me to do.

Faith with practice goes a long way…Journey on Babe…

Figure 21. 2016 George Petronella post fight with Jody.

About the Author

Jody-Lynn Reicher resides in Northern Bergen County New Jersey with her husband of nearly now thirty-three tears and their two daughters. Jody-Lynn has a background in the military (USMC), also working in the financial and accounting fields in corporate environments for ten years before becoming Licensed Massage Therapist and ART practitioner for medical purposes.

She started her therapy practice nearly twenty-five years ago. Recently, she began teaching part-time, private, self-defense lessons for teenage girls and women.

Jody-Lynn still holds the North American Women's 24 Hour Treadmill Record, as this book goes to press, she's third in the world for that same distance. She has run nearly 500 events of middle distance, long distance, marathon distance (forty-one), and ultra-distance (forty). She has ground fought ninety-five matches, and fought nineteen stand up matches.

She's done several speeches on life's lessons and struggles, physiology, and athletics. She is the author of "The Endurance Athlete's Guide to Nutrition" (2006), soon to be revised. "Reaching God's Perfection...Stories of Gratefulness" (2014), "Priceless in Changsha" (2017).

Her upcoming titles of her next Books: "How to Ruin a Pearl", "Journey On Babe...How to Liberate a Woman", and "Writes of Passages, Stories in Prose".

Figure 22. Mr. Steve Bratter, Boxing Trainer at YESS.

70124793R00188

Made in the USA
Columbia, SC
05 May 2017